The Little Book on EMF

My personal journey through the *EMF Balancing Technique*®

Lina Esposito

"... Long ago,
with wax-wings, Icarus flew blindly
towards the sun,
and being soul-less fell.
But here, climbing the creaming cloudfall,
my silver thread
collects the dew-pearls of all the mornings of
my life
and whirls them, flashing moon-fire,
through my head. ..."

To my father, Peter Esposito,
who has taken his soul's next step.

Foreword by Peggy Phoenix Dubro

When I first met Lina Esposito, I was impressed by her very presence and potential. It has been a joy watching Lina grow into the confident young woman she is now. I have great memories of the time we co-taught an EMF Balancing Technique practitioner training in London, England. Working together, along with her partner Michael, I had a beautiful experience with two caring individuals giving of themselves in a joyful and open manner. We worked together in such harmony; a demonstration of what is possible when there is true peace-filled empowerment.

I am honored to be part of Lina's life and her journey. To dare to become what you know is possible always takes persistent acts of courage. It is always meaningful to have those who support you in this process of persistence. Of course, in the interacting energy of the figure eight, she is also part of my process of becoming! Lina shares her heart in this little book in a big way. I hope you will take the time to feel the heart and the support behind the story.

One of the messages of the EMF Balancing Technique is to encourage one another to experience and demonstrate a greater and greater sense of wholeness. This message, when spoken in the language of energy means, "I believe in you and your wholeness, your wholiness!" This energetic message speaks to the very core of an individual and the results of this experience can be profound and life changing. Human to human, we energetically support one another in the co-creation of our most enlightened life.

As mentioned earlier, it has been a pleasure watching Lina grow into who she is now - mother, teacher, and author, sharing her experience and encouraging others to grow also. I look forward to watching her continue to shape and define her potentials according to her ever increasing wisdom!

In the energy of love,

And as always,

Peace filled empowerment,

Peggy Phoenix Dubro

Acknowledgements

Thank you Peggy Phoenix Dubro for your courage and dedication in bringing this unique work to us. Thank you for modelling integrity - it shines forth from you. When you enter a room and begin to speak, I am touched by the energy of pure love.

Thank you Stephen Dubro for your unstinting support and guidance and for always being there with your insightful wisdom. Your strength and calm is an example to us all.

Thank you both Peggy and Stephen for your love and trust in me.

Thank you Michael, my life partner, for your unconditional love and acceptance. Without you, I would not be who I am today.

Thank you Maria for your help with this book.

Thank you Michael Oliver for always being there to encourage me, understand me and make me laugh.

Thank you dear Shana and Ilan for your sheer hard work and constant support.

Thank you dear Greig and Lorianne for pointing me in the right direction and for your unique and enduring friendship.

Thank you to all my fellow EMF practitioners and teachers who are out there spreading the energy in the way Peggy desires.

Finally, thank you to all my clients and students for placing your trust in me and for teaching me so much.

Foreword

In early 1999 I was suddenly overwhelmed by a powerful urge to get out of the depressing and unfulfilling rut I had been stuck in for many years. I began a conscious search for personal transformation and self-fulfillment which led me to the EMF Balancing Technique®. I was deeply unhappy when I began, yet now I have inner peace, self-empowerment and direction in my life. I was a spiritual novice when I began, yet now I have a good understanding of how to achieve spiritual fulfillment. This book is about my journey - where I began, the routes I took and my final destination.

My wish is that my story will show you that you can transform your life and become the person you would like to be. No matter who you are or where you start from, you are not stuck, you can take control, you are free. Change is possible and it doesn't have to involve suffering. This idea was completely new to me and very exciting when I began my journey and I now know from personal experience that it is indeed true. Right now we are living in extraordinary times when personal transformation can be faster and more graceful than ever before.

My biggest enjoyment has been discovering and working with the new energy, watching it in action with hundreds of clients and students as well as in my own life. The new energy is one of co-operation - competition no longer works - and one of pure intent: things happen quickly for us if what we desire is for the collective good as well as our own. It also involves a very respectful and non-invasive way of interacting with others, empowering them and honouring who they are rather than seeking to change them.

Using this technique over the past five years has helped me evolve into a conscious person - I am conscious of my words, emotions, thoughts and actions and the effect they have on myself and others around me. Of course, it means that I have to constantly be aware of this, and take responsibility for everything, which is a very different kind of life for me, but one I enjoy as it is very empowering.

2004 finds me at home, a full-time mother to Theo, my one year old son. I used the technique to release fear, balance my hormones and relieve stress during my pregnancy with wonderful results and I continue to work regularly on myself and on Theo. The work has had a stabilising effect on me - I feel as if I have good, solid foundations and the inner strength to face any challenges that may occur in my life. Of course, the challenges continue to change and evolve too as I grow, but I have plenty of tools to work with. One of the most practical things I have learned is that I am not perfect and don't always react as I would like to, but I keep on practising and remain positive - one day it will change. My immune system is strong, my dramas are few and far between and I feel abundance in every area of my life.

My understanding of who I am and what I am here to do continues to evolve. Right now my role is that of a mother to Theo, to guide and nurture him, to give him the tools so that he may live a fulfilled and empowered life. My responsibility has deepened a hundred-fold - Theo makes sure that I continue to put my spiritual principles into action and practice what I preach!

I have taught the EMF Balancing Technique to over 150 people. What I love most is to watch people light up and I share their excitement at finally finding a way of taking control of their lives and making positive changes. This has given me great hope for our planet and for mankind - we can change ourselves and we can change the world around us. In these unusual times, this information has given me a much needed overview of recent world events.

I wrote this book about the impact of Phases One to Four of the technique on my life. Phases Five to Eight are now available to work with and they mark an even deeper level of empowerment for us. Knowing how far the first four phases propelled me forward personally, I am looking forward to experiencing this further step forward and am very excited to see what this next stage brings me.

What I have learned is that old ways are no longer valid in these new times we live in. A momentous shift is taking place right now not only in energy work and spirituality, but also socially, geologically and politically. We are all at a critical turning point in our personal and collective history. All of us are involved in this and right now, more than ever, we can take part and make a difference. The EMF Balancing Technique has shown me how. And so I take that opportunity to create a peaceful revolution in myself, for my fellow humans, for my planet.

Lina Esposito
London 2004

Table of Contents

Awakening

The Early Years

I was born into a working class Italian family - my paternal grandparents emigrated to the UK from southern Italy during the late part of the nineteenth century, built up their family business and settled into a pleasant house in a respectable, leafy north London suburb. My father was born in 1935, the youngest of five children. For my grandparents, my father was an unusual and difficult person. From a very young age he was an unruly free spirit - he did not like to be tied down and he often got into trouble. He was very bright intellectually, a would-be poet and an artist with an interest in spirituality. As someone who enjoyed life and the artistic and cultural aspects of London, he did not fit into the expectations of society in the 1950s, and especially not those of a rigid Roman Catholic Italian family. When at the age of thirty he was still living at home, without a suitable regular job and getting into scrapes with English women, my grandparents decided it was time for him to get married and took steps.

Returning to Italy for a family holiday one year, my grandparents made enquiries and found for my father what they considered to be a suitable southern Italian bride from a local village - my future mother. My mother and father were introduced and after a couple of meetings, they were married. Having been born into a poor southern Italian farming family, my mother had received a minimal education and life for her had been hard. After marrying my father she left her family behind for London, moved in with my grandparents and began her married life, hoping that life would change for the better in England.

It was a strange marriage. My mother did not speak English, my father only spoke a little Italian and so communication was minimal. They had nothing in common. She knew nothing about the world whereas he had travelled, read widely and experienced more of life. His outlook on life was open whilst hers was rigid and closed. Living with his dominating parents meant that they had no privacy. Unsurprisingly, my father did not spend much time at home. Life was stressful for my mother; stuck at home with parents-in-law she didn't know or like. She became extremely sad and longed for home. In 1966 I was born into this challenging marriage. I did not see much of my father and spent most of my time with my mother and grandparents. This meant that the first language I was exposed to was Neapolitan, a dialect of southern Italy. My first words were in this language and I continued to speak it until I went to nursery school, when I very quickly picked up English and stopped speaking Neapolitan.

As time went on, life in my family became more difficult. In time, we moved out from my grandparents into a small home of our own and my sister was born. My father was finally forced to face up to his responsibilities, take on a manual job in his father's business and support his family. It was not what he wanted. Over the years he became more and more disillusioned with his life and withdrew from us. He was angry and frustrated at his situation in life and became bitter and cruel towards my mother. As the years went by and he never managed to find the courage to change his situation, he also became miserable. He did not want to be with us and he was often vocal about this to my sister and me, telling us that if he could start his life again, he would never get married and have children. As my sister and I grew up and began to have opinions of our own, he became much more verbally abusive towards us. Conversations with him were always highly charged emotional affairs and tended to consist of aggression and competition - he was always right and we were always wrong. It was impossible to speak to him rationally and eventually I gave up. I had lost my voice.

Meanwhile my mother also became more and more miserable - she seemed to always be ill and became a submissive and fearful wife. As a result there was a lot of tension in our family home. We dreaded my father coming home in the evenings. Anything could trigger his troubled emotions and so we were always nervous of him, always on tenterhooks. Every year we would go to Italy for our summer holiday and spend time with family and friends. I looked forward to this - it was an escape from life at home and I enjoyed playing outside with my cousins and friends and being part of their community. We ran and swam and ate and got up to all kinds of mischievous activities. The air was pure and hot and we ate lots of good, hearty fresh food. It was a time of innocence and fun, countryside, mountain and seaside. It became my second home.

As I grew up and moved into my teenage years, I found being caught between two cultures very challenging and I struggled to express myself. I was beginning to explore vegetarianism, environmentalism, free thinking, human rights issues and I was also developing my own unique clothing style. But my mother had brought her repressed, overbearing and inflexible rural Italian Catholic values with her and I was obliged to conform to them. I was not free to be myself and I felt misunderstood and trapped. I developed no self-confidence. I was quiet and shy at school and although I had a lot to say, in class I preferred to listen. If I was asked a question, I would blush and stammer and my mind would go blank. I wasn't used to being allowed to have an opinion.

As a teenager I developed an interest in religion and began to go to church of my own accord. I enjoyed it and I felt uplifted and joyful at the end of mass. I took Religious Studies at 'O' and 'A' Level and was considering studying Theology at university. I remember at one point I even considered becoming a nun! However, I somehow became disillusioned with my religion and then I discovered boys and that was the end of that!

Desperate to leave my suffocating and miserable home, I thought the only way out of my predicament was marriage.

So at the age of twenty I married my first real boyfriend. Unsurprisingly, there were difficulties in my marriage right from the start. Very soon it became apparent that I had recreated the same patterns as my parents: my husband began to behave like my father had and I was turning into a frightened, frustrated wife. My marriage was fast becoming a replica of my parents'. I felt suffocated and after a couple of difficult years, I broke free, promising myself that I would never again allow my freedom to be taken away from me.

Over the next ten years, I went from relationship to relationship. I fell in and out of love. I was very quickly bored and I couldn't manage to be part of a stable relationship. If things were going well and seemed to be stable, I would begin to feel tied down and I would somehow destroy it. I was not proud of the way I was behaving but I couldn't seem to help myself; I felt out of control. Part of me secretly enjoyed the roller coaster ride of emotion and drama.

I moved from flat to flat, never living anywhere for more than a couple of years, never really feeling at home, never having time to settle in before I was on the move again. I was always in work, but I was always short of money. I spent a lot on going out and enjoying myself, paying for luxuries and holidays and my wages would disappear quickly. Over the years I became more and more reckless. I took more and more risks and I became entangled in all sorts of unhealthy situations. I was smoking and drinking a lot. On the surface it seemed as if I was having a great time, but inside I was sad and depressed. I had an emptiness inside that was growing and growing and nothing seemed to fill it.

Having studied English Literature at university, it was a natural progression for me to teach. I enjoyed my work and ended up teaching for ten years. Teaching satisfied my communicative, intellectual and creative needs, but being sensitive to the needs of every student and putting every drop of my own energy into my work left me exhausted. I became drained, regularly took time off work due to illness and eventually I was obliged to resign because I was completely burnt out. I then tried out a variety of other jobs. I went from job to job, searching for fulfillment, but it always seemed to evade me. Although at first I would enjoy my new work, it soon bored me and I was on the move again. Both my self-esteem and my self-confidence were low - I felt that I was no good at anything.

My relationship with my father was virtually non-existent and he had absolutely no interest at all in my life. He was ashamed of both my sister and me - we would never make anything of our lives, he told us. My relationship with my mother was poor. It had suffered due to my divorce and patching things up with her was a long process. The emptiness inside me seemed bottomless and unfillable.

By the beginning of 1999, many things in my life were coming to a head at the same time. I was living at home with my parents, I was short of money and lacking privacy. I had trained as a make-up artist and was working for a well-known and respected company. But I found the work to be stressful, exhausting and boring and I was often ill. I was also in an unsatisfying and unfulfilling long-distance relationship, which was going nowhere. Emotionally I was unstable, I was frequently unable to face the world. It felt as if everything in my life was collapsing around me and I was powerless to do anything about it. I needed a miracle.

The Miracle Happens

One morning at work during a break I sat drinking a coffee with my colleague, complaining bitterly about my life. My colleague looked at me and asked "So what is it that you would really, really love to do?" No-one had never asked me that before. I considered the question, looked straight back at her and said "I want to help people, I want to be a healer." I didn't know where those words had come from, I had never said them before. They had just spilled out of me, but they felt right. My friend smiled and said "You know, I can really see you doing that." "Really? Can you really?" I asked her, needing confirmation. "Yes I can", she replied.

As we made our way back to work, I felt very excited about my revelation and began to feel warm inside. As I did my client's make-up, she commented, "You must love your job, it's so glamorous." "Actually, I don't enjoy it at all. I want to be a healer", I found myself replying. That was the second time I had said that in less than half an hour and this time I said it with conviction. "Well, how about something like aromatherapy? I'm an aromatherapist", asked my client. I considered this and instinctively answered, "No, I don't want to work directly on the body." "Well, how about Reiki or some form of energy work? I'm also a Reiki Master", my client suggested. Energy work - that was it! For the rest of her make-over I asked her lots of questions and she provided me with a list of books to read and ideas to research. As she left she said to me, "It is no coincidence that I am here today. When the student is ready, the teacher arrives." I never saw her again but that short conversation was to change my life.

For the rest of that day I was in a dream. People asked me what had happened, told me that I was suddenly glowing and that my voice had changed. I knew that I was finally on the right track.

I felt lighter inside and I finally knew what it was I really, really wanted to do!

Now that I had a purpose, I couldn't think about anything else. I went through the motions of going to work but all the while I was thinking about energy work and helping people. I read spiritual magazines and scanned the lists of the different complementary modalities available. There were so many of them, but none of them appealed to me at all. I visited spiritual shops, read a few books and made some enquiries at various schools of healing. Still nothing appealed. Around the same time my sister moved into a two-bedroom flat and asked me if I wanted to move in with her. I said yes and took a couple of weeks off to move and go on holiday. I ended up going alone to a country cottage set in a wood just by the coast in Yorkshire. On my second day the telephone rang. It was a lady who worked as a crystal healer in a house nearby. She had heard that someone was staying in the cottage and she wondered if I wanted a session. I had never experienced anything like it so I decided to go and see her the next day. At the end of my session she looked at me and said "You are going to do some sort of energy work and you're almost there". She mentioned that she was holding a Reiki workshop in a couple of month's time. Would I be interested? It was the second time in a couple of weeks that someone had mentioned Reiki to me. I said I would think about it.

Back at work a few days later, I again went for a morning coffee break with my colleague. This time a friend of hers joined us and during the course of our conversation, she told me that she had just done a Reiki workshop. A bell rang in my head. This was no coincidence - it was the third time I had heard Reiki mentioned. I knew I had to take action! I asked her to write down her teacher's contact details. She wrote a telephone number and the name Michael Bennett on a piece of paper.

By now there was a sense of urgency about it. I was propelled to call Michael Bennett. I told him that I had to learn Reiki as soon as possible. He didn't seem surprised by my demand and we made arrangements for my Reiki 1 training. When the day arrived I turned up at his front door and rang the bell. While I was waiting for him to answer the door, it crossed my mind that I knew almost nothing about Reiki or energy work, and Michael Bennett was a complete stranger. What was I doing here? I had no idea what to expect. A young man with olive skin, dark eyes and a gentle demeanour opened the door and let me in. He spoke softly and he was incredibly calm. I was the only person on the workshop that day. The day flew by as I listened intently to what he taught me.

As well as learning Reiki that day and becoming aligned to the energy through an attunement process, I learned about unconditional love, the existence of energy in the universe and energy fields. Michael taught me that peace and joy were my true nature and I could use energy work to touch that state within me again. He also taught me that everyone is a part of the whole and that the universe speaks to us all individually and personally all the time. He introduced me to the concept of a non-judgemental and loving Creator, of which I was a part.

I learned how to give myself a Reiki treatment and so the day ended. I went home with a whole new vision of my life and the universe! I had enjoyed the day - I liked Michael's non-dogmatic approach. The next morning I woke up with a profound sense of peace and stillness. For the next week took I every opportunity to use Reiki on myself, morning and evening and even during breaks at work if I could manage it! I kept expecting this new peaceful state to disappear, but it didn't. In fact, the more Reiki I did on myself, the more peaceful I felt. The next week I returned to finish my training, alone again. By the end of the day I knew how to treat others and I had learned how to use the energy in my every day life.

Now that I knew how to give energy sessions to other people, I intended to give them whenever I could and there were plenty of opportunities. Everyone at work was eager to try it out and I would often spend my breaks giving people short treatments. Wherever I was, people would ask me for a quick treatment and I always gave them one. At home, I gave my sister treatments every day. People I worked with had definite sensations and experiences of the energy. This gave me confidence - there really was something going on! I enjoyed working with the energy and kept giving myself and others treatments every day.

A few weeks later on the Tube on my way to work, I caught sight of a fine band of colour surrounding the person sitting opposite me. I looked around at the other people in the compartment. I could see it around them too. Everyone had a different colour! The colours were beautiful, some subtle, some luminous, some flourescent. They had a different quality and luminescence about them and were unlike any colours I had ever seen. I looked around in amazement, smiling! All day at work I stared at people as they went by - I could still see the colours! Over the next few weeks I saw more and more colours. Sometimes I could see layers of colour. They were alive, bright and pulsating.

My heart always gave a little jolt when I saw them. It felt as if what I was seeing was truly precious.

As I worked with the energy, I would have definite sensations in my hands. Sometimes it was intense pain, as if I was being stabbed in the palms, sometimes a dull ache, or a buzzing or a prickling. At other times, I would feel a gentle tingling or intense electrical surges that took over my whole body. Often I felt a strong magnetic force pulling at my hands. Every time I worked with the energy, I experienced a wash of love through my whole body which brought tears to my eyes. Michael Bennett had taught me that the Reiki energies were the energies of unconditional love and I was beginning to experience that for myself physically and emotionally.

I went about my daily life, but I had a new perspective on everything. Work receded into the background. Things that had bothered me before were suddenly no longer important. The unsatisfying and draining long distance relationship I had been in for almost a year, which had been a constant source of emotional stress and upset to me for so long, didn't seem to worry me any more. My focus had shifted.

Six weeks after my Reiki 1 training, I took the next level. Reiki 2 marked a complete turning point in my life. I woke up the morning after my training and knew that I was going to change everything in my life. I instinctively knew that the time had come - it was now. It was the moment for me to take action. I had no fear or doubts. In fact I wasn't even thinking or reasoning. It was an instinct that was both forceful and real. It was a direct knowing. That morning I remember hearing the doorbell ring very early. I opened the door and was presented with a beautiful big bunch of flowers. It was from my boyfriend. The card attached said "Congratulations on your Reiki 2". It was the first time he had given me flowers but I was not excited or overjoyed by them. As I looked at them I realised that it was over between us. I felt calm and detached. At work I went about my usual way but I felt different. The usual stresses were not affecting me, I felt almost invisible and glided around doing my work, quietly, in a detached manner. I felt free. I felt alone. I felt relief. Inside I was saying goodbye to everything and everyone there. At the end of the day I knew that my work was over. I never went back. Later that week my relationship was over. I had no regrets. I was free! I had let go without any fear and my universe was about to change.

The World of Energy

The next morning I began to have new and wonderful experiences. I felt intense surges of electrical energy coursing through my whole body. The sensations were incredibly intense, almost painful. It felt as if every part of me was being shocked into electrical action. I was buzzing! It was a little uncomfortable, but I didn't mind because something incredible was happening. Then I began to feel as if someone was pulling very fine strands out of me all over my body. I could feel very fine filaments tugging at my skin and unravelling. Sometimes the tugging was so strong that my body would twitch and I would often feel the skin on my face being physically pulled this way and that. Around my face, above my head and beneath my feet, the sensations were particularly intense. I could often feel something sitting above my head, moving around! It was as if something new was forming all around me, like a network or a web.

Over the next few months, I made changes in my life and let go of inappropriate relationships and unhealthy habits. My health improved and I decided to devote myself to energy work. I was living with my sister and it was a safe and nurturing environment. We were both out of work, both at home and we had fun. We laughed a lot, we sang and danced, we did creative things, we supported each other. It was like being children again and

I felt so relaxed and carefree. I was in the perfect space for my spiritual transformation.

My time was now my own. I went out and bought books about energy and spirituality, buying the ones I was instinctively drawn to. I spent my time reading and applying what I learnt to my life. All my waking hours I meditated and did Reiki on myself. I bathed myself in the energy of unconditional love twenty four hours a day. I applied myself to actively practising the concept of unconditional love with the people and situations in my life, past and present. I had a steady stream of insights, and after each insight I made the changes I felt were necessary so that I could continue moving forward. I also let go of the things that were holding me back - habits, addictions, old ways of being. Each time I let go and actively made changes, my experience of energy got deeper, my perceptions were heightened and my understanding of myself and my universe sharpened. I went higher and higher. I could feel my resonance changing. I was living inner peace and strength. I knew that I was loved by the universe - I was in bliss!

One day I gave the intent to learn and experience more and see more of the universe. My intent was fulfilled for that day was the beginning of an intense period of insight and revelation. Every day, for the next six months I saw - with eyes open - more and more energy of varying colours and shapes. I saw the Flower of Life symbol hover in front of me. It was enormous, brilliant white and static but the geometric patterns within it rotated and mutated fast. It would appear as a circle first and then the patterns within would form themselves in front of me.

Brilliant violet and white musical notes made of energy would stand in front of me six foot tall and I would hear a note in my head. I then began to see - still with my eyes open - huge, vibrating, luminous light patterns spinning all around me. They were vast - as large as my room! I saw huge circles gently bouncing all around me like large bubbles. I also saw many small circles within larger circles rotating slowly in front of me, like a dial. There were large, bright, shining figure of eights sitting quivering quietly beside and in front of me, reaching up to the ceiling. Three dimensional diamonds, some with many facets, some simple, presented themselves to me, as if greeting me quietly. Catherine wheels of energy exploded all around me, filling my room with beautiful coloured light. Complex ever-changing and mutating geometric patterns would spin fast and furiously all the way around my room.

There was a powerful silence in the room but their presence was potent. They were very real. Although they were made of light, they were also in some way solid. I watched the displays with awe and felt a powerful energy of love and peace when I saw them. Although it was overwhelming and at times almost frightening, it was really magical. I looked forward to seeing them every day and made sure I had hours of free time to devote to watching them. Although I had no idea what these were or what was happening, I felt that somehow these were part of me, but I wasn't sure. These experiences went on for months and became part of my every day life. And I loved every minute of it.

I wondered what all this meant but nobody I spoke to seemed to have a plausible answer. There was a big question mark within me. Despite this it was a very special time. The days merged into each other and I had a feeling of timelessness. I was in the middle of a huge and intense learning experience. I never knew what each day would bring me. What would I see today? What would I learn about myself and the universe today? What synchronicities would happen today? It was an exciting game!

Having no-one else to talk to about my experiences, I began confiding in my Reiki teacher, Michael Bennett. He seemed to understand and was always there to listen and advise. Seeing my dedication and intense experiences with energy, he invited me to be his assistant. I was thrilled! I had nothing else to do and the thought of being in the energy was exciting. So twice a week and sometimes more, I would make my way to Michael's house and assist him on all of his workshops. I heard the information over and over again and soon I knew it by heart. I watched the attunement process, whereby the Reiki teacher helps the student to open up to the Reiki energies, I received and gave sessions. It was a profound time for me and I learned a lot about energy.

In some of the books I had read that energy was channelled through the crown of the teacher and then passed on to the student, but as I sat quietly in the corner of the room and watched the attunement process, I saw something else happening. The energy appeared in the room from every angle - from above, below and all sides - and it bathed each person. It was not coming through the crown of the teacher and going out through his hands into the person. It was everywhere! It was more concentrated in some areas than in others and it was bathing everyone according to their needs. The energy was alive and pulsating. It moved and glowed and shimmered. I saw different shades of different colours appear and move around the room. Sometimes it would bathe the person totally, moving towards them and through them and around them, like a shiny, scintillating cover.

Soon I was seeing this energy everywhere. On trains, in cafes, in the street and in shops, I would see billowing clouds bathing everything. A new world within my world had opened up to me and every day I gave the intent to see even more about energy and the workings of the universe. And I was not disappointed! New experiences would come every day or two, opening up my consciousness to new possibilities. I felt as if I was on a magical guided tour of a new reality. My life had been turned upside down in a short space of time and I knew that nothing would ever be the same again. I couldn't go back from here. I could only go forward.

Walking home from Michael's house one summer day, I looked up at the buildings and saw a glistening energy all around them. When I looked around me at the trees, people, cars and shops, I noticed that they were also framed by the same quality of energy. At that moment I had the realisation that everything was made of a similar stuff. At home, I looked around my flat. Everything had a glistening, pulsating alive frame around it. The experience was incredible. The energy framed everything, much like a frame outlines a picture, but I could see that there was a depth to it. It wasn't just external; it seemed to be originating from within and radiating outwards. There was so much activity with everything moving, pulsating and shining. I was experiencing a universe buzzing with life and it was exhilarating!

During this time, despite having no job, I didn't have one moment of fear because I felt cradled by the universe. Everything I needed always came to me at just the right time in the most miraculous ways. I was existing on virtually nothing, but after a while I began to be concerned about money and I applied for work. I very quickly found the perfect temporary part-time job in central London. On my first day of work, I opened my purse. There was only three pence in there and I had nothing left in my bank account! I did not panic because somehow, I knew that I would be fine. It would take hours to walk to central London, so I carefully worked out when I would have to leave. However, just before I was due to leave the post arrived and in it was a completely unexpected three months overdue payment cheque! I cashed it, gratefully. That cheque tided me over the next couple of weeks until I got paid. I saw it as more proof that I was not alone: I was always looked after by the universe. 'The universe' became a concrete reality for me in those magical months and it still is. I always trusted it and I was always provided for.

Over those months I spent a lot of time with Michael. He was my teacher, confidant and advisor. To me he was a wise and gentle teacher - he taught me everything I knew about energy. I admired him because to me he was an example of how it is possible to live what you teach with integrity and love. Energy work was his passion and he had followed his dream, turned it into a reality. As time went on, and I described my experiences of energy to him, he also began to learn from me and our relationship progressed to a more equal footing. Soon we were friends, getting to know each other and spending time with each other. One day as I was getting ready to go to Michael's house, I thought about him and suddenly a vision of us together flashed vividly through my mind. It was accompanied by a strong emotion of love in my heart and great excitement throughout my whole body. At Michael's house a while later, I suddenly saw him in a whole new light and I realised I had feelings for him. Michael obviously had those same feelings for me too, for not long afterwards we became a couple. I was so happy - our intent was to base our relationship on unconditional love and integrity and still is. It was my first healthy, honest and unconditional relationship. Part of me fleetingly wished that I had met Michael years before, but I realised that I had not been ready for this kind of relationship until now. I was now who I was supposed to be, I had resolved many of my concerns around relationships and made the appropriate changes in my life. Many people called me 'lucky' to have such a partner. Yes, I was fortunate, but I believed we came together because of the paths we had each followed and our willingness to change our lives. We had worked on ourselves and followed our dream, and ultimately we had both created this.

I loved Reiki. It had changed my life overnight. I trained to teacher level but somehow I was never drawn to teaching it. Instinctively I knew that there something else coming for me, something different that would suit me perfectly. It would excite me and fulfill me. I gave intent to find that.

An Answer

My experiences with energy continued and still I had no explanation. So, one day Michael suggested that we put out an intent to the universe for some answers.

A couple of days after putting it out, Michael was out in London with a friend and decided to visit an esoteric bookshop. Whilst browsing in the shop, he noticed a young couple. He smiled at them and they smiled right back. Michael was struck by the kind and gentle way they were interacting with each other and also by how particularly bright and happy they looked. Michael then went downstairs - there they were again. He had an urge to talk to them, but resisted it. Just before leaving the bookshop, Michael joined the queue to pay for his books and as he looked round he noticed that the couple had joined the queue directly behind him. Michael again felt a strong desire to talk to them, but again resisted the urge, left the bookshop and headed off with his friend to a particular café for a cup of coffee. Unable to find the café, they headed back to the main street. Standing in the middle of the street, apparently looking for something, was the young couple! This time there was no hesitation. Michael approached them, introduced himself and struck up a conversation. The couple seemed open and friendly and he invited them to his house for lunch the following week. The next week they met up as arranged and enjoyed their time together. Michael told me that he had met a very nice couple and he wanted me to meet them too. So not long afterwards, I found myself in a London café chatting to Greig and Lorianne, a very relaxed and loving couple newly arrived in town from South Africa. They were on my wavelength and I immediately warmed to them both. I felt very comfortable with them and soon I was telling them about many of my experiences.

When I had finished telling them, Greig looked at me and said "There is a book you should read". We finished up our drinks and headed for the nearest esoteric bookshop. Greig selected a purple book from the shelf, opened it up and put it into my hands. I looked down and saw a drawing of a human body with a structure around it. I felt a rush of excitement and my whole body began to tingle. It was as if time stood still - everything receded into the background. At that moment there was only the book and me. The drawing was new to me but somehow I recognised it. Above the drawing were the words 'The Universal Calibration Lattice'. Here was the new network - it was a lattice! Here were the strands radiating out of the body! There really were large structures above the head and beneath the feet! As my eyes moved towards the top of the page I read 'The EMF Balancing Technique'. EMF stood for electromagnetic field - for months I had felt the electricity throughout my body and the magnetism in my hands. Here were the swirling energy patterns all around. The universe had answered my request. As I looked down at that page, my experiences all suddenly made sense. I looked at the front cover - it was called *Letters from Home - Kryon Book Seven*[1]. I bought it.

When I got home I began to read the purple book. The chapter on the EMF Balancing Technique enthralled me. A strange sensation overwhelmed me as I read. In this chapter Peggy Phoenix Dubro describes the technique she developed as "tracing crop circle patterns through the human energy field". When I read that sentence my heart lurched and I knew that this was what I was going to do. This was the energy work I had been waiting for! Everything that had happened in my life had been leading me towards this point! I went online to the main worldwide EMF website and came across an exercise called the Spiral Sweep. I read through the text, visualising each movement as I went along. When I came to guiding energy through my creative/sexual centre, it felt as if that part of my body was actually starting to come alive. I felt a surge of energy, excitement and joy. It felt so strong and so tangible. I was taken aback at how strongly my energy had responded

1. The author of the Kryon book series is Lee Carroll – see www.kryon.com for more information.

and I took it as another confirmation that this work was right for me. I clicked around the website, reading everything I could. I saw that there were practitioners and teachers all over the world in many countries and that it was spreading fast. I wanted to become a part of this! I looked at Peggy Phoenix Dubro's schedule and saw that she was coming to Europe, to Paris, to teach a practitioner workshop a few months later. Michael and I booked on. And I couldn't wait!

I began to reflect on the past few months. I thought back to that cold February morning when I had first had the sudden realization that helping people was my vocation. My life had changed so dramatically in such a short space of time, and now, just eight months later, I had found my way. We didn't see Greig and Lorianne for a while - they had decided to travel around Europe for a few months. I was so grateful to them for showing me the way and I hoped that I would see them again.

Around a month or so before the training, after we had invested our money, a slight doubt appeared in our minds. We were going all the way to Paris for a week to learn a technique we didn't know too much about. Were we doing the right thing? We had a strong relationship with the universe and so we decided to ask for a clear indication of whether we were on the right track. That day, we went out to central London. As we were going down an underground station escalator, someone going up the other way flicked a small piece of paper. It flew across and landed next to Michael's hand. Michael flicked the piece of paper down the central divider of the escalator. The piece of paper tumbled down. As we travelled down the escalator, we again reached the piece of paper and again Michael flicked it and again it tumbled downwards. Just as we got to the bottom of the escalator, the piece of paper suddenly flipped over next to me. As I went past I caught a glimpse of it. It was a theatre ticket for a play and the play was called *Peggy for You!* I grabbed it. We were both amazed! This was the sign, the final confirmation!

I kept the ticket for quite a while afterwards, marvelling at how the universe is always on our side.

Revelation

A New Part of My Being

And so one afternoon in mid-May 2000, Michael and I boarded the Eurostar high speed train in London and travelled to Paris to take Practitioner Training for Phases I-IV with Peggy Phoenix Dubro.

Michael and I were very early on the first day so we took our seats and waited in anticipation. I was curious to see Peggy Phoenix Dubro in the flesh! Finally, a well-dressed blonde woman walked into the room and took her place at the front of the class. She introduced herself and began to teach. Peggy was gentle, friendly, down-to-earth and approachable and she had a great sense of humour. She was the originator of the technique and her energetic presence was palpable. Yet she had a certain modesty - this was no guru! I warmed to her immediately.

I sat and listened to Peggy describe a newly evolved part of our energy anatomy called the Universal Calibration Lattice, or UCL. As she spoke she drew each part on a whiteboard. I scribbled down everything she said and carefully copied the diagrams into my notebook. Peggy explained that the UCL is made up of fine fibres or strands of energy that begin within the core of the being and radiate out from the energy centers (or chakras), to form a latticework structure around the physical body. As I noted this down in my notebook it dawned on me again that here was the explanation for the tugging sensations I had been experiencing all over my body. I had been feeling the fibres of my UCL forming!

When Peggy came to the end of this part of her presentation, I looked up at the whiteboard and saw the UCL - the whole UCL. Suddenly my whole body was overcome with a powerful emotion of recognition. Here on the whiteboard in front of me were the geometric light patterns I had been seeing - my beautiful magical shapes! At that moment I realized that for all those months I had been seeing with my physical eyes the patterns of my very own electromagnetic field! I had been witnessing the activation of my Universal Calibration Lattice. Tears began to well up. I was feeling in my body an emotion I had never felt before. In retrospect I can look back at that poignant moment and see that the energy coursing through my whole being was my very first experience of the energy of pure love. I tried to hold back my tears, but the feeling was too overwhelming and for the first of many times to come, I allowed myself to cry.

Peggy took the time to describe the structure and functions of the Universal Calibration Lattice to us in great detail. She told us about electromagnetic fields, explaining that wherever there is a moving electrical current, an electromagnetic field is naturally created around it. This is a scientific fact supported by many studies, especially those of pioneering scientist Dr Robert O Becker. In his books "The Body Electric" and "Cross Currents", he shows how the human body runs on electricity. Our brains function by means of electrical impulses, which also course through our nervous systems, sending messages. There is also research to suggest that each and every one of our cells produces an electrical current, implying that an electromagnetic field naturally occurs around each individual cell. The latest research hints that this is the way that our cells communicate - by sending electromagnetic information signals to each other. As our cells have a surrounding electromagnetic field, then our body too generates a collective electromagnetic field, which is the sum total of all our cells. In the past, before such scientific research had been done to verify the existence of electromagnetic fields, people referred to this phenomenon as the human 'aura'.

There are many scientific books written about the human electromagnetic field, as well as many written by those who can see and sense this part of the human being. There are many facets to it and, just like the human physical body, it is made up of many different parts or systems. The Universal Calibration Lattice is one system within the human energy anatomy.

I was very attracted to the way Peggy was explaining this. I liked the scientific aspect; there was nothing mystical or strange about it. Instead, it seemed very real and down-to-earth.

The Universal Calibration Lattice

The physical body contains many systems within it, such as the skeletal, the endocrine, the nervous and the muscular. In the same way, the human energy anatomy contains many systems within it. These include the meridians, a network of energy lines and points along the human body which can be unblocked and balanced during acupuncture sessions. Other systems include the chakras, the energy vortices along the body. These energy centres are one of the ways in which we interface with the energy of the universe and much of the ancient knowledge about this system is now being rediscovered. In many well-known practices such as yoga and Tai Chi, people perform various movements to unblock and energise these vortices. There are also other systems such as the emotional, mental and spiritual energetic bodies which surround our physical body. These too have been explored by many people.

Recently, a new system has formed within the human energy field as part of a collective leap forward in human evolution. Around fifteen years ago, after many years of spiritual seeking and study, Peggy had a very profound and personal experience with this new system and has dedicated the intervening years to researching, documenting and working with it. She has named it the Universal Calibration Lattice® (UCL). Given that all the separate systems within the energy anatomy are interconnected and work together harmoniously within the body, working with one system will naturally affect all the others. Any work with the UCL will therefore have a knock-on effect on the other energetic systems and the physical body.

The UCL, then, is a newly evolved part of the human energy anatomy, of ourselves. Thanks to the efforts of those practising spiritual modalities in recent years, the consciousness of humanity as a whole has taken a significant step forward. One aspect of this has been an acceptance of increased empowerment and a willingness to accept greater responsibility for ourselves and our lives - a readiness to graduate to the next level of spiritual maturity. The appearance of the Universal Calibration Lattice within our energy field reflects this leap and working with it enables us to begin to make use of our new level of empowerment.

The UCL is made up of very fine golden fibres of light and energy. It begins from a central core that runs through our body and radiates out to a distance of around 60cm/24 inches away from the physical body. These fine fibres radiate outwards from the energy centres (chakras) and form themselves into infinity loops, which connect to other parts of the UCL.

The Centre Above and the Centre Below

Above the crown, infinity loops connect to a large energy centre 60cm/24 inches above the crown, named the Centre Above. This centre connects us to our higher wisdom or understanding, to the higher, more refined energies of our being. The infinity loops beneath the feet connect us to our Centre Below, 60cm/24 inches beneath our feet. Through this we are connected to and communicate with the energy of the earth.

The back fibres

Infinity loops radiate outwards from the energy centres behind us and connect to long vertical fibres of light called the long informational fibres. The long informational fibres are also 60cm/24 inches away from our physical body and they connect to both our Centre Above and our Centre Below. These long fibres contain discs of light and energy which hold the records of our personal history, including other life information, hereditary patterns, genetic traits and all the events of this life. They also hold information about our strengths, talents and abilities from this and other lives.

These discs function like transmitter-receivers so that if there is an excess charge of energy relating to an event in our history, that energy transmits out to the universe. This energy is then attracted back to us magnetically, bringing with it events, experiences, situations and people which shape our reality. As long as the excess charge remains, it continues to attract similar events, experiences, situations and people to us, creating repeating patterns in our lives. When we learn from these experiences, the excess energy is released, travels via the infinity loops and comes into our Now time. This provides us with more available energy for us to use in our daily lives. The lesson we have learned is then recorded as wisdom on the discs behind us, which means that there is no longer any need to repeat that particular experience.

As we take the opportunity to learn from all our life experiences and view them as events containing particular wisdom to help us grow, so we accumulate more and more knowledge in the back fibres of our UCL. In this way we gradually build up a gleaming column of wisdom and support behind us, which we can draw upon in our daily lives. This leads to greater self-reliance, self-sufficiency and self-confidence. We begin to find strength from within.

We can also begin to activate the wealth of hidden talents and latent abilities recorded on the discs behind us, providing us with the talents and skills to move forward in our lives. As we do this, we find direction in life from within ourselves.

The energy patterns within the back of the UCL remind us that we really do create our own reality every moment and that we are responsible for our own lives. We now have more empowerment to change our lives as we release old energy that may be holding us back. We can begin to shape for ourselves the reality we would prefer.

The Core Energy

The Core Energy is a central column of energy that runs the entire length of our being, connecting us to our Centre Above and Centre Below. It represents the Now time. As we strengthen and balance the Core Energy and begin to radiate it outwards, we begin to feel more inner peace, unconditional love, well-being, in fact all those characteristics we would associate with mastery. We affect all around us with this energy. The Core Energy is also the place within our being that provides us with the answers we may need in our daily lives. The more we get in touch with this part of ourselves and practise living in this posture, the more self-trust we develop and the more we realise that we are masters!

The side fibres

The infinity loops also radiate outwards from the energy centres on the right and left side of our physical body. They connect to long vertical fibres which also contain discs of light and energy. These discs contain information to do with the balance of our giving and receiving. Those on the right transmit the energy we give out to support people, places, groups and events in our life. Those on the left are designed to receive the energy of support from the universe, from people, places, events and groups. Balancing the charges on these discs enables us to form a more balanced relationship with the universe in our daily lives, as we give and receive more equally. In this way we are able to take more control and give our energy to those projects and people of our choice, rather than just allowing our energy to go out unconsciously. We can also begin to feel more supported as we open ourselves up to receiving more.

The front fibres

Infinity loops radiate out from each energy centre in front of us and connect us to the long informational fibres which are 60cm/24 inches in front of us. The discs within these long fibres hold the energy of our potentials - our hopes, dreams and projects, just waiting for us to explore. They also hold the energy of fear and worry about what we refer to as 'the future'.

The front fibres of the UCL are the dynamic place of co-creation within our being. Co-creation is the process of working in partnership with the universe to bring our wishes into reality. We transmit our intents to the universe from the discs in front of us and attract energy back to us via the front fibres to support us in our projects, helping to bring them into reality. The front fibres provide us with our very own personal dialogue with the universe. With a fully-formed UCL in place, we can make use of our more mature and equal relationship with the universe and co-create the things we would like in our lives in a whole new way. The presence of the front fibres of UCL also reminds us that we are worthy of all the things we wish for - we have earned that right. Dreams and intents can become a reality much more quickly than ever before.

Evolving new parts

The exciting thing about the UCL is that it is dynamic and constantly evolving, just as we are. New fibres holding fresh information are being activated and there is still much more to come, allowing us to grow and awaken new aspects of ourselves.

The Cosmic Lattice

Another exciting aspect of the UCL is its unique connection to the Cosmic Lattice. The Cosmic Lattice is a lattice-like structure which permeates the entire universe and existence. It holds all the unlimited, creative energies of the universe.

It is through the activation of our UCL that we set up our own personal and permanent connection to the Cosmic Lattice. Through the use of our UCL we begin to tap into the Cosmic Lattice, drawing upon its vast energies to use in our daily lives. Our UCL makes our individual and important presence in the universe much more strongly felt - much like putting a loudspeaker to your energy field and stating "I am here"! And because our UCL has its own unique resonance, the Universe can reply to us more quickly and personally than ever before.

All this means that we can co-create things more efficiently in our daily lives, making us more active world players and enabling us to join in the universal scheme of things. We are basically more connected.

Later that morning Peggy explained that humans beings are composed of carbon, chemicals, electricity and light. At this point in our evolution, we are activating more of our electrical nature. With that explanation I finally understood why I had been experiencing huge surges of electricity throughout my body! My excitement rose. The request Michael and I had made to the universe six months ago was being answered and I was so grateful.

As the day progressed, I could feel a joyfulness bubble away inside me - I was smiling inside! Here was a whole new dimension of myself to learn about and I loved it. Peggy respectfully asked us to set aside the word 'aura' and to replace it with 'energy field' or 'electromagnetic field'. 'Aura' can still have mystical connotations for many people, she explained, and now that science is beginning to study and document the existence of energy fields, these new words and ideas are more accessible and acceptable. She also asked us to replace the word 'psychic' with 'intuitive', as the word 'psychic' may also sound mystical and can give the impression that only certain people are gifted in this way. The word 'intuitive' refers to another of our senses, just like touch, smell, sound, sight and hearing. Just as we all have our other senses, so all of us can intuit too. I liked what Peggy was saying - this was a whole new language and it resonated with me.

Back in my hotel room that evening, I looked through my notes from the day. The afternoon had provided us with a variety of practical exercises: some to strengthen and balance our UCL and help us evolve, others to co-create things we would like to have in our lives. We had learnt how to work on ourselves and how to send energy to help others. The day ended with learning how to give a Mini Session, a short 10-15 minute session given to someone sitting in a chair. In just one day I had taken so much life-changing information away with me and had many new tools to try out. This day alone had been a life-changing experience for me. The existence of the UCL was an exciting reality for me. I had felt it and had seen it.

I felt privileged to be learning this unique and up-to-date information. I looked at my diagram of the UCL. Here was a clear, practical visual of the mechanism within my energy field that explained such ancient universal spiritual truths such as the answers are within you, you create your own reality, you reap what you sow, you are a powerful co-creator. It was such an empowering revelation! This information had a profound impact upon my understanding of myself and my life. And I was looking forward to working with it.

Phase One - Balance Wisdom and Emotion

The next morning I awoke fresh and ready to go. After yesterday's session, I was excited about what the day would bring. The morning began with Peggy and other teachers facilitating an energetic alignment for us and alignments continued to take place throughout the training.

Alignments

The ability to work with the EMF Balancing Technique is passed on from the teacher to the student through an alignment process. Teachers are specially trained to do this and it can be likened to the way a tuning fork works. When one tuning fork is vibrating and another tuning fork is placed next to it, the second tuning fork will vibrate at the same frequency as the original tuning fork. I was familiar with the idea of alignments as they are a similar kind of process to Reiki attunements, which enable the student to open up to the Reiki energies.

Peggy explained that she had developed the EMF Balancing Technique as a structured, systematic way of working with the UCL. The technique consists of sessions called 'Phases', which each have an overall intent and focus on a specific part of the UCL. Each Phase builds upon the previous one and so a client always begins with Phase One.

The Opening Ceremony

Each session begins with the Opening Ceremony: "From the Creator within me, to the Creator within you, and the company we keep, let us begin". The beauty and power of those words immediately struck me. They honour the Creator within all of us and honour the fact that we are all equal in this respect. I could also see that the words stated right from the very beginning that we were going to be working with each other from that higher place within ourselves.

The Company We Keep

"The company we keep" refers to any help that is present during the session. Our company does not intervene, it merely observes and supports. Peggy explained that the emphasis in this work is on the human-to-human connection. We, as humans, are doing the work ourselves. Our company stands by in a supportive posture. It seemed to me that what Peggy was saying did not apply only to the session. It was exactly the same principle in every day life. I could see that this concept marked a new level of empowerment for us. Now it is time for us to stand in our own power as humans. We make our own decisions and do the work ourselves.

I began to think about the company that we keep all the time, not just during sessions, and about what I had heard people refer to as their 'guidance' from other sources. I knew that I had for many months been regularly seeing what people called 'other dimensions' or 'other beings' but I wasn't sure what I really felt about this. What Peggy was implying resonated with me very strongly. I was happy to go within myself for the higher wisdom and act upon decisions made by myself, all the while knowing that I was being supported.

"From the Creator within me, to the Creator within you, and the company we keep, let us begin". How different and wonderful the world would be, I thought, if we all interacted with each other in this way!

A New Way of Working

That afternoon, Peggy demonstrated a Phase One session. I watched her perform graceful, fluid movements around someone's energy field and say certain words aloud. It looked like a beautiful dance. She seemed to be tracing different patterns through the energy field and although the general feel was very fluid, the movements had definite beginnings and stops. There was a definition about them that I liked. The words that I heard seemed to somehow "fit" the movements. I had never seen anything like it and was fascinated. I couldn't wait to try it myself!

Peggy explained that the aim is to perform the movements as gracefully and evenly as possible, avoiding any bouncing or shaking of the hands or sudden breaking-off. This is because as the practitioner's hands move through the UCL, a resonance is created to which the client's energy responds. Their energy then begins to rearrange itself into the next pattern of balance. Any deviation from the set pattern interferes with this process and so lessens the effect.

The session itself seemed to be made up of a sequence of these movements and words (known as 'say alouds'). It was put together in a certain way and had a very real structure, which also appealed to me. I instantly understood and respected that there were reasons why they were being performed in this way and it made sense that it was important to keep the sessions intact. It was obvious to me that Peggy Phoenix Dubro had spent many years lovingly perfecting these movements and intents. What I understood was that using her understanding and sight, Peggy had put together a specific series of movements which when performed precisely and done in a certain order, had a profound effect upon this part of the energy field. It was a universal pattern to which each of us would respond uniquely, according to our inner wisdom. Peggy asked us to follow this set pattern and with the same integrity and respect I sensed she had shown to us and to the technique, I decided there and then to faithfully adhere to it.

The New Energy

Practising a technique of energy work with form and structure resonated with me very strongly and I felt very comfortable with this way of working. I remembered reading in *Kryon Book Seven - Letters From Home* about the recent evolution in the collective human consciousness and the magnetic shifts in the electromagnetic field of the earth. The whole paradigm of energy work is currently in the process of changing. The energy of the earth has changed - in the book this is called the 'new energy' - and different vibrations of universal energy are available for us to work with. Because of this shift new techniques and completely new ways of working are also becoming available. As I watched Peggy perform the session, it struck me that the EMF Balancing Technique is one of these new ways of working, the next generation of energy work for these changing times. It is the next big step forwards. I felt privileged and very excited to be a part of it!

From my Reiki work, I was familiar with the idea that universal energy is a spectrum of different vibrations, much as light contains a spectrum of colours, each with different characteristics. The new energies we were to work with have the following attributes: they are self-regulating and self-directing. This means that they are directed by the inner wisdom of the client according to their needs at the time. Also, the ability to work with them is gained by an energetic alignment from the teacher. They also resonate specifically with the UCL. I was looking forward to learning about and exploring these new energies for myself.

Templates of Light

Peggy explained that tracing the pattern of the Phases through the UCL awakens specific energy patterns within the energy field called 'templates'. Each Phase awakens a specific template. The templates are patterns of light and energy forming three-dimensional diamond shapes. We all hold templates of light and although they look the same in everybody, the geometric energy patterns and information within them are unique to each person. This is very much like our hands - the shape of everyone's hands is similar, yet we all have unique fingerprints. Our templates resonate with each of our potentials, our special gifts and abilities. We all have something unique to offer and our templates transmit and receive information about this, helping us to discover why we are here and what role we have to play.

Phase One

Peggy explained that in Phase One we were going to begin working with the fibres of the UCL. The specific movements of the technique draw out the fibres and connect them. This opens up channels or pathways within the UCL, so that the energy can flow more freely and smoothly. We were going to work on the front and back fibres, as well as those which connected us to our Centre Below to help us to feel more grounded and present in our body. She also explained that each Phase has an overall intent and the intent for the Phase One session is to balance the wisdom and the emotions. I could appreciate the importance of this when I reflected back on my life and realised that I had made my life decisions based on either my heart or my head, providing me with far too many adventures I was not keen to repeat! The way forward was to use both in equal balance.

Having learnt all this exciting information, I was eager to actually perform a session. That afternoon, I had my first opportunity. It felt very much like doing Tai Chi. I found myself moving gracefully around my partner's body, guiding universal energy through their UCL. Some movements were easier than others - but this didn't worry me. I knew that with practice, I could perfect them. Saying aloud the words was a completely new experience for me; it felt a little unusual, but I enjoyed it. The energy itself was very gentle and refined - definitely different from anything I had ever felt before - yet also incredibly tangible.

After receiving a session from my partner, I sat up with a feeling of inner stillness and stability. I felt very present and alive. There was so much more to learn, and though I didn't have the vocabulary or the experience to describe it yet, I already felt different.

Phase Two - Self-Direction and Self-Support

The next morning we learnt more in-depth theory about the back fibres of the UCL. Peggy explained that during the Phase Two session that afternoon, we were going to be working through the back portion of the UCL. This is the part of the UCL that holds the records of our history. We were going to give the intent to release excess electromagnetic energy from our history that may be holding us back. This released energy would then recycle back into our UCL, providing us with more energy to use in our lives right now.

A New Paradigm of 'Karma'

I thought about what Peggy was saying to us. I had read about the concept of 'karma' in spiritual books, which explained that the unresolved energy of our other lives continues to impact on us by creating similar life 'lessons' again and again in subsequent lifetimes. The implication is that if we do not learn these lessons, we have to continue to re-experience them again and again until we do learn. I remembered references to being caught in the 'wheel of karma' and the importance of suffering to the full the same incidents before we can learn and move on. I had found the concept a little suffocating. It gave the impression of being trapped in a cycle of events beyond my control and sounded like hard work.

Graceful Release

But Peggy was now describing a whole new concept. She explained there was no need to relive the original experience of our history as we released it. When working with the UCL with this technique, we can choose to take the wisdom of the experience without reliving the 'heavy' lessons or painful emotions. There is no need to suffer in order to grow. The released energy is recycled back into healthier energetic patterns in our UCL. The evolution and presence of the UCL in our energy field and the ability to work with it means that we no longer have to release energy in a cathartic way. I had experienced for myself a couple of other modalities where release involved 'catharsis' - that is, expressing, analysing and reliving old emotions in order to transform them and move forward. I could understand that this way of doing things may have been appropriate for other times, however, one of the characteristics of the 'new' energy is that release can now be more gentle and balanced. The new vibrations of energy are different and are more graceful and empowering. I felt a huge sense of relief as I heard this - it felt so liberating. The whole paradigm of 'karma' had changed! Here again was evidence of a new way of working. I was beginning to understand more about the concept of the 'new energy dynamics' and the enormity of its implications for us as evolving humans in these new times.

Peggy was also using the term 'other' lives, moving away from the idea that these were past lives. This replaces the notion that time plays out in a linear fashion and supports the idea that all we have is the now. I liked her terminology. Peggy's language was neutral. She spoke about releasing and rebalancing excess energy in our history in order to gain wisdom. She made no mention of 'negative' or 'positive' energy and encouraged us to move away from the idea of 'good' and 'bad' energy. She asked us to view our history as a potential source of wisdom and support, not as baggage. I liked these ideas - I found it a much more positive and empowering way of looking at my colourful history!

Self-Regulating and Self-Directing

Peggy explained that the energy of this work is self-regulating and self-directing, which means that the recipient's inner wisdom determines the result of the session according to their needs at that time. The practitioner is merely a facilitator who follows the pattern of movements and then steps back and encourages the recipient to trust that their inner wisdom is directing the whole process. The practitioner focuses on balance for the recipient. There is no diagnosing, analysing, or commenting on another's energy. To me this sounded so empowering and so unobtrusive, especially for the recipient. We were going to just allow people to be who they are and not try to 'fix' them. In my personal life I have always been passionate about respecting each individual's personal, sacred space and aim to be tactful and gentle in any advice or opinions I give. I have never been keen to interfere in other people's lives in general, so I was happy that as a practitioner I was to continue in this way. I had also experienced other people commenting on my energy before and did not feel comfortable with it as it felt so invasive.

Furthermore, the practitioner uses universal energy, not their personal energy, and so there are no personal energy exchanges between the practitioner and the recipient. So as universal energy flows through both, both receive the benefits of the session. What a wonderful idea, I thought: giving is receiving!

A New Way for Our Times

I liked the word 'practitioner' rather than 'healer' and I was beginning to understand that an EMF Balancing Technique practitioner is not a 'therapist' or 'healer' in the usual sense of the word. This new way of working is different to the conventional idea of therapy where things are analysed and discussed and to the idea of visiting a 'healer' who 'heals' you. I could appreciate that much of the old terminology no longer applies. As old concepts are changing, so new words and new ways of expressing fresh ideas are being formed. This is a natural and organic process, a part of life. As the workshop progressed I began to appreciate more and more the incredible evolution taking place in energy work.

Being 'In Service'

That morning, I began to think about the relationship between the practitioner and the recipient. So far I had learnt that practitioners are facilitators, allowing the recipient's inner wisdom to determine the outcome of a session. This also implies that the person receiving the session is in fact the one who is directing the process, with the help of the practitioner. The practitioner is not 'doing anything to' the recipient. They are both working together, co-operatively.

I also began to reassess the meaning of the word 'healing'. In this technique, I had learned that the practitioner always focuses on balance, and it made sense that things have to fall into balance first before any other benefits can take place. And when I thought about it, I realized that 'healing' can take place in more ways than one. It can happen physically, mentally, emotionally or spiritually and we cannot predict which way it will occur.

All in all, it seemed to me that we are in the process of redefining what it means to be in service to one another. We are in the middle of a momentous shift in the relationship between client and practitioner. My spirit soared! Everything I had learnt so far was so refreshing. I felt grateful to be able to work in this new way and have access to this empowering information.

Phase Two

In the afternoon, Peggy demonstrated Phase Two, which was a more in-depth session. Part of the session involved working along the spine, releasing specific energy patterns called restrictions. These hold in place energy that has been with us for a very long time. This energy creates important life experiences for us, giving us the opportunity to learn lessons. Once the lesson is learnt and the restriction is released, a whole new level of well-being is reached. As I watched the respectful sequence of movements, I began to really understand why there was structure. Working through the UCL layer by layer, the structure ensured that the release and rebalancing was gentle and nurturing. I could see the importance of this and how it allowed people to stay in balance and strength when working on such a deep level.

The overall intent for Phase Two is self-direction and self-support. The session helps us to release old patterns that may be holding us back. Practitioners work through the fibres of the UCL at the back, opening up and balancing the energetic circuits so that energy can be released smoothly and efficiently. As we learn from the experiences that arise, the energy of our history is transformed into usable wisdom that we can draw upon in daily life. This helps us feel more confident in our ability to support ourselves and leads to greater self-reliance as we find more strength from within. The session also helps to activate latent talents and abilities, to access those qualities that take us to where we would like to be. This gives us more direction in our lives. How amazing, I thought, and practical and useful. To be able to tap into all our accumulated abilities to help us in our lives here and now!

As I gave a session to my partner, I found that the movements already felt much more familiar and more comfortable, even though only a day had passed. I felt more confident. And for the second time during that week, I again felt the overwhelming rush of energy throughout every cell of my body. There was a feeling of pressure in my high heart area accompanied by a sensation I now recognised - the energy of pure love. Tears welled up again - it was so tangible! The energy of love was not just a theory - it was real.

I left feeling very excited. The idea of releasing old repeating patterns that had been holding me back for so long without necessarily having to relive pain sounded wonderful and completely plausible. I fully understood the implications of what I had learned that day - this is a new paradigm of energy work. I was honoured to be a part of it.

Phase Three - Radiating Core Energy

On day four we looked at the Core Energy in more depth. The Core Energy is a central column of energy that runs the entire length of our being from the Centre Above (60cm/24 inches above the crown) to the Centre Below (60cm/24 inches below the feet). I remembered these energy centres from the first day of the training: the Centre Above is our connection to our higher consciousness or higher energies and the Centre Below is our direct connection with the energy of the earth.

Peggy showed us how to make a connection to these two parts of ourselves. It was a fast and easy technique: there were no long meditations or lengthy processes. I was taken aback at the speed of it. Now that the energy of the earth has shifted, things can happen much more quickly for us!

The Core Energy is the place within us where we find peace, strength, balance, compassion, joy and many more characteristics that have long been associated with those we call 'masters'. It is also where we can be in the 'Now' and it can provide us with all the answers we need in our lives.

Peggy taught us an exercise to connect with our Core Energy and to radiate it outwards all around us, into our lives and into our entire universe. I experienced an immense sense of peace and solidity doing the exercise and I particularly enjoyed radiating my Core Energy out into my entire universe. I could sense it reverberating in every direction, allowing me to be heard like a resounding call. It made me feel a part of everything. I felt as if my energy was affecting the whole universe. This is who I really am, I thought, at my core. It helped me to remember this. It felt so good that I wanted to be this in my daily life more and more. The simplicity and practicality of the technique appealed to me. It can be done anywhere from a mountain top to a bus queue, Peggy explained. Simple, fast and practical - I loved this technique!

Mastery

I began to think about the attributes of 'mastery' within myself and what it meant to be spiritual, to be a 'master'. I wondered how I could reach that goal. I had read and heard many opinions on this matter ranging from sitting in silent meditation on a mountain top to fasting or following a spiritual guru. Peggy's answer was one simple word: practise. Practise your peace, your compassion, your joy, your patience, your non-judgement. Practise anything that means mastery to you in everyday life with everyone and everything you come into contact with. I understood what she was saying. When I thought about my life, I could see that it provided me with all the experiences appropriate for me to practise being a master of my own life. And Peggy assured us that even though we may not always behave according to our highest standards, we need not worry as another opportunity for us to practise would always come along. I felt relieved. There was no need to be perfect all the time and no need to be hard on myself. I could remember who I was by practising a simple technique.

Core to Core

I knew and believed the concept that the Creator is in each and every one of us equally and I had tried to look for this part in everyone, no matter how they were behaving. It hadn't always been easy. But looking at the picture of the UCL, I now had a clear visual of where to look for the best in everyone I met - the Core Energy. I could imagine what it would be like to interact with someone as we both radiated our Core Energy. One person would not dominate the other as we would both have our own connection to the universe. We would treat each other with respect, each empowering the other, reaching a deeper level of communication. And even if one of us was not connected to their Core Energy, the radiating of the Core Energy of one would inspire the other to do so. Communicating core to core - I immediately knew that this too was all part of the new energy dynamics. It was a new way of being with one another.

As Above, So Below

Looking at the picture of the UCL, I could see that the Core Energy connected us strongly to our Centre Above and Centre Below. This connection enables our higher energies to flow down from our Centre Above, through our Core Energy and down into our Centre Below. This enables us to hold and experience our higher energies, or our 'spirituality', within our physical bodies. The flow down to the Centre Below anchors those energies all the way down into the energy of the earth, helping us to feel much more present and giving us a spiritual purpose. I could see how focusing on and strengthening our Core Energy would help us to bring our higher energies into our bodies, our biology. As above, so below.

The Marriage of Spirit and Biology

Peggy explained that the aim of the technique is to help people experience their spirituality in their body right here and now in everyday life. This led me to thinking about how important the physical body is. I thought back to one of the say alouds in Phases One and Two - "The key to freedom is to be fully present in your body". In much of my reading the importance of spirituality was emphasised, but not that of the body, as if the physical body is a lesser part of us. I felt relieved that this technique was encouraging me to reconnect with and feel comfortable in my body. My body is the vehicle that holds my spirituality; it is not a separate part of me and I understood that both the physical body and spirituality need to merge in order for us to feel whole. This is what is meant by the marriage of spirit and biology, I thought.

This technique seemed to me to be about being here, being present in your body here and now, in this world. It was about being human. It was about being the best you can be in this society, at work, at home, with friends, family, work colleagues, and partners. It wasn't about sitting for hours in meditation to achieve a certain state of consciousness. It was about practising living the most enlightened life you can here and now every moment of every day. I liked it - it all sounded so grounded and achievable.

The Answers are Within Me

The Core Energy is the place where we go within ourselves to find the answers we need. In class that day we learned a quick and easy exercise to access these answers. I realised that there is no need to go outside of ourselves - everything we need to know is all there waiting for us to access. Having spent much of my life being unsure of my own judgement and my ability to make good decisions, this was good news indeed. It felt very empowering and I could see that the more I practised this, the more I would trust myself. I could also see that this process also involved learning the new skill of discernment in order to make balanced and healthy decisions. I was keen to begin doing this. Yet again, this work was placing emphasis on the empowerment of the human being, as he or she begins to rely on the higher aspects within him/herself. I remembered my thoughts from the first day about the company we keep. Here was a way to honour that company for its support and yet stand on our own two feet. I could see that this too was an evolution, another aspect of the new energy dynamics.

Radiating Outwards

At no point did Peggy mention protecting yourself or closing down. Instead, we learnt how to radiate our Core Energy with strength and balance outwards. The more we radiated that resonance out, said Peggy, the stronger we would become and the less things would affect us. I had always been so sensitive to everything and everyone around me and this had often overwhelmed me. But here was a way to strengthen myself without shutting down or separating myself from other people. It was a way that was empowering both to myself and the other people. Radiating outwards - it was all part of this new way of being with others in the world.

Balance Not Healing

Having heard all this information, I again began to consider the concept of healing and what it meant in this context. As I thought about Core Energy and what it would be like to live in that energy, I could understand even more why this technique is focused on balance and not healing. Living in your Core Energy means that you can connect to your inner strength and knowing. It means you can experience balance and inner peace, no matter what state your physical body is in. This was about how to achieve inner well being, I realised.

Give and Receive in Equal Balance

That day we also reviewed the side fibres of the UCL. Peggy reminded us that the discs within the fibres on our right hand side is where we give our energy out to the world in support of people, places, things and events. The discs in the fibres to our left is where we receive the energy of support from the world. We learnt a simple exercise to call our energy back from supporting people and situations we felt may be draining or inappropriate. This exercise also showed us how to open ourselves to receive more support from the world. Doing this creates a healthy balance between what we give out and what we receive. As I looked back at my life I suddenly understood why I had so often felt tired and drained. For years I had been unconsciously giving too much of my energy in inappropriate ways and not allowing myself to be supported. What I learned that day was a complete revelation to me and I promised myself that from now on things were going to be different. I was going to become more conscious of my energy and actively choose where to send it to. I had learnt a tool that would give me more control over my life.

Phase Three

Peggy explained that the intent for Phase Three is radiating Core Energy. That afternoon we were going to clear the smaller energy vortices (chakras) around the body that lead into the larger ones. These small vortices include the areas around the joints, such as the knees, hips and jaw, where a lot of tension is often held. As the energy here is freed up, it results in a greater flow of energy into the major energy centres. We were then going to activate the flow of energy from the Centre Above to the Centre Below and vice versa, unifying all these energy vortices into the core. Finally, we were going to strengthen the radiating of the Core Energy and guide each other in radiating that energy outwards into our entire universe.

That afternoon I found myself performing lots of circling movements. It was a very thorough session - I worked around the front, back and sides of my partner as well as above and below them. I became very aware of my body as I stretched and moved. It felt as if I was exercising my body too. I could see that the benefits of being a practitioner are physical as well as energetic. I would need to become more flexible, but I knew that practising the sessions would help me do this!

I felt at peace with myself and my world that evening. I was happy - I had found a modern spiritual technique for accessing the nobler aspects within myself and I had a way of getting in touch with the answers within me. I also had a whole new and empowering way of communicating with others. I was beginning to piece together exactly what being and working in the new energy was all about. Now all I needed to do was practise.

Phase Four - Energetic Accomplishment and Potential

When I awoke the next morning, a part of me was sad - I was enjoying myself so much and now I was coming to the end of the course. Over the past few days I had met some EMF Balancing Technique teachers who had been using the technique for a while. They looked peaceful, glowing and comfortable with themselves. Working with the technique, they had all developed their own personal experience of the UCL, becoming more and more aware of it. Some had seen or felt parts of it.

Co-Creating in The New Energy

That morning we looked at the front fibres of the UCL. The discs within these fibres hold our potentials - our hopes, dreams, wishes and projects - and also our fears and worries about our future. This part of the UCL is where we have our very own personal conversation with the universe about what we'd like to create in our lives. When we have an inspiration to make something happen, this energy is transmitted out through the front of the UCL. The universe then replies to us, again through the front of the UCL, with a sign or synchronicity to let us know that we are on the right track. The next step in the process is to take action. It is this action that sends another wave of energy out through the UCL that the universe can respond to, leading us to the next step. As we continue to note synchronicities and take action, we work together with the universe to turn our dream into a reality.

I knew the concept of creating our reality with our thoughts and intents and had worked with affirmations before, but this was going one step further. This was active and dynamic. It involved being alert, taking action and more responsibility for our lives. And we were using a new and different part of our being that connected us more potently with the universe, allowing things to happen more quickly. There was no element here of whether we are worthy or not to have the things we would like - it was implicit that we are indeed worthy. I remembered reading in the Kryon book that humans have graduated into a deeper and more equal partnership with the universe, working together for the good of the whole. This is all part of the shift into the new dynamics and looking at the UCL, I could see that now I could really begin to take part.

Co-Creating with the UCL

Peggy showed us a simple procedure using our UCL in a structured way to create what we would like in our lives. We firstly reached behind us for wisdom and strength from our history. Then we centred in our Core Energy, making us very present and finally we reached forwards in our UCL and planted specific intents in front of us. We also connected to our potential self, a part of ourself who may have already created that wish, and asked for guidance on how to go about creating that reality.

I was amazed at the effectiveness of this technique. It felt very potent and focused and the structure meant that it was not just a vague wishing for something. I had a good visual - I knew where to go within myself to focus my consciousness. I was using the structure of my energy anatomy, not just my mind. It was very empowering to feel that I was creating my own potential. I became aware of the increased power of my own thoughts and actions - I'd have to make sure that I used this new level of empowerment wisely! I could understand what Peggy meant when she said that our 'futures' are not necessarily fixed and cannot necessarily be predicted any longer. We have a choice of potentials in front of us and we are now creating our own reality as we go along, moment by moment. Our 'future' is in our own hands.

Going with the Flow

I could see that there was no need for me to struggle to create what I wanted in my life. It was a case of planting intents in the front of my UCL and taking action when the universe sent me back a synchronicity. It was also about not struggling with intents that were clearly not flowing for me - going with the flow was very important.

I remembered the many years searching for something that would inspire me and make me feel fulfilled. I knew how it felt not to have a path in life and how this could lead to depression and dejection. I realised that the front fibres of my UCL, the part of myself that holds my potentials, had not been fully formed and activated. I had a feeling that this was all going to change for me very quickly now and I couldn't think of anything more wondrous than offering a technique to others that would help them move towards their dreams too.

Phase Four

The intent of the Phase Four session is energetic accomplishment and potential. We were going to work through the back fibres of our partner's UCL first, encouraging them to have gratitude for all the experiences that had brought them to this point and to access the wisdom they had gained along the way. Then we were going to help our partner to connect with all the benefits of their Core Energy. Finally, we were going to work through the front fibres, completing and activating the front of their UCL. This would open them up to their potential and allow them to plant their intents and wishes in front of them. I could see just how interconnected the UCL is: working through the back affects the sides and the front. Each fibre affects all the others.

I did not have the words to describe how giving the Phase Four session felt that day, but it was mainly a feeling of sacredness. As I helped my partner to open up from deep inside to their own potential, I felt as if I was blessing them. Every movement felt special.

When it was my turn to receive the session, I was very aware of the words that were spoken to me. The words explained how I could empower myself to move forward with my life by letting go of long-held patterns holding me back. They reminded me of my strengths and talents and the many potentials that awaited me. They also reminded me of my power - I felt uplifted and optimistic. It was obvious to me that those words had been carefully chosen to allow for the deepest response. I felt their impact and, as I listened and followed along with my practitioner, I felt as if I was participating in the process.

Keeping the Technique Intact

Before the end of the workshop, practitioners of other modalities wanted to know how they could best combine their other work with the EMF Balancing Technique. Peggy's answer was clear. She told us that she preferred it if clients avoided receiving other energy modalities around the time of their EMF sessions. In this way, they could experience the technique fully and be able to distinguish its unique benefits from those of other modalities.

Knowing that the EMF phases were a specific series of movements and words that had been put together in a specific way for a certain response, Michael and I had no intention of combining the technique with our other work. We were going to keep our other work completely separate. What Peggy said made perfect sense to me. I wanted to make sure that my clients received exactly what they had come for. To me this seemed part of the respectful honouring and empowerment of each other.

On those last two days we also learnt a few more tools: how to give distance and phone sessions and how to treat ourselves. At the end I was reluctant to leave, but our train was waiting for us and so we sped off to the station, boarded the Eurostar and headed back home.

Homeward Bound

Sitting on the train on the way back to London, watching the French countryside flash by, I was quiet and pensive. In my mind I was replaying the events of the last six days and digesting everything I had learnt. The thing that excited me the most was learning about the recent momentous shift in the energy dynamics of the earth and how this affected my life. Using my UCL, I could now speed up my spiritual evolution and transform my life without necessarily having to suffer heavy lessons. I felt privileged to be able to take advantage of a new deeper and more mature relationship with the universe. This shift involved more responsibility on my part, but it also meant that my potential was in my own hands. It all added up to more self-empowerment.

I had learnt about the part of my being that held my history with all my repeating unresolved patterns as well as all my talents and abilities. I had also learnt about the energy of my giving and receiving and my potential. I had a variety of techniques and exercises to work with on myself, and I had tools to help others as well. There was no dogma, no rules to follow and no conditions - this was just a technique to help me grow into the most fulfilled person I could be. I realised that this was what Peggy had meant by a technique of self-empowerment and self-enablement.

It felt as if a door to a new beginning had just been opened up for me and I was standing on the threshold of something that would change my life forever. Feelings of excitement and expectancy bubbled up; life had taken on a whole new meaning for me. Already I felt different and everything looked different. I had no idea what was going to happen but I knew that whatever it was, it had enormous significance. I had a sense of something sacred beginning and the feeling was overwhelming.

Transformation

How We Got Started

All Change!

Michael and I arrived back home late on a Friday evening, on a real high and incredibly energised. So energised, in fact, that we got up very early the next morning, cleaned the house and taught a two day Reiki workshop!

That morning, I found myself offering to teach a part of the workshop. Michael had often asked me to do this before but I had always been too afraid, feeling more comfortable just being his assistant. Yet that morning a new confidence emerged from within me. For the first time, I felt no fear. I suddenly felt as if I was now quite ready and capable. The part I taught went very well; the students listened to me respectfully and accepted me as their teacher. That day I felt quietly amazed at myself! I had achieved something that until then had seemed too daunting to even try and I had done it well. At the end of the weekend I felt completely different. I was no longer Michael's assistant - I had redefined myself. Although I had only taught a part of the workshop and Michael had been beside me, it was a real breakthrough for me. I was now a Reiki teacher. We had only been back from Practitioner Training for two days and already my life was changing. I started to get the feeling that I was capable of doing a lot more than I had previously imagined. The training had begun the process of activating my potential and this was just the beginning, although I did not know that then.

It was not only internal changes we noticed. At that time we were living with between two to four other people who also ran a teaching practice from the house. As our housemates were paying most of the rent, they naturally had more use of the teaching space and we had been sharing the space with them, slotting in our workshops and sessions around their timetable.

A week or so after we got home from practitioner training, our housemates informed us that they had decided to move out and within a month, they had gone. Michael and I were amazed - this had come out of the blue! Finally, the whole house was ours to expand into. For the first time we had a dedicated session and teaching space all to ourselves! Everything was changing fast so we could hardly believe it! We knew that this signified the beginning of our full-time EMF Balancing Technique practice and I knew that this marked the beginning of my career as a professional EMF Balancing Technique practitioner. I was redefining myself further. We had learnt on the training that the technique was a system that helped us to move into our potential, but we hadn't expected it to work so quickly.

I thought back to the training and wondered how all this could have happened in such a short time. Throughout the six day training we had performed energy exercises, done meditations, given and received sessions and learnt all about a new part of our energy anatomy that held the key to awakening our potential. The result was that our energy had rearranged into healthier and more balanced patterns. We had released old energy that had previously been holding us back and had activated talents that we could use to move forward in our lives. Our balance of giving and receiving had evened out, and we had moved into a deeper, more equal partnership with the universe. During the training our UCLs had been balanced and strengthened, activating our potential and increasing our self-worth. When I remembered all the energetic work we had done, it all made complete sense that within a month of the training everything around us should change.

Practising

Having seen such positive changes for ourselves, Michael and I immediately began to practise the sessions on family and friends, offering them for free and taking every opportunity that arose. We did the sessions together. While one of us performed the movements, the other spoke the say alouds and following the practitioner manuals, checked and corrected any mistakes. In this way both of us had the opportunity to review and practise all the movements and say alouds and gain a good basic understanding of all the sessions. Michael and I intended to keep the integrity of the work intact and by doing it together this way we ensured that we were doing the sessions exactly as we had been taught, without changing or adding anything or missing anything out.

Meanwhile, little miracles began to happen. At a party one evening, Michael demonstrated the energy by moving his hands over someone's palms without touching. This person had had a spinal injury which meant that she was not able to use one of her hands. As Michael performed this movement, she said that she could feel tingling and electricity going up her arm and shortly afterwards she miraculously picked up a glass of beer with her previously unusable hand! We were all taken aback that such a simple movement could have such a profound effect so quickly. This energy worked on the physical too!

Preparation

During this time, I began to read my way through the list of books that Peggy had recommended and any other related books I came across. I did this slowly and carefully, making sure that I was taking everything in. I made notes as I went along and recorded any insights I had about the technique whilst reading. I reviewed all my notes from the training and wrote them out again. I also recorded experiences and results from the sessions we were giving to family and friends. I became a serious and dedicated student of the EMF Balancing Technique. Deep inside I knew that it was essential to do this. This was my work and I intended to study it thoroughly. I wanted to make sure that I understood what this technique was all about and how it benefited people. During this time the technique was often on my mind, and I soon began to make connections.

A Daily Practice

I had also made it my priority to practise EMF daily. I knew that it was not enough to merely take a workshop. I felt that in order to benefit and grow from a technique it was necessary to practise and integrate it into everyday life. And I knew that this was a process; it required dedication and persistence. Every day I gave myself a session and I also chose one of the many meditations and energy exercises to do. I also recorded my own experiences. In this way I was able to incorporate the energy into my daily life and build up my own personal experience and understanding of the work.

Explaining the Technique

Having gained some experience and done some reading, I sat down to think about how I would explain the EMF Balancing Technique to people. I thought carefully about what made it different to other techniques. To me the work was unique because it had been specifically developed to work directly with the UCL, a newly evolved and accessible part of everyone's being. I could think of three other reasons: the movements themselves were unlike any I had ever seen, the energies had particular qualities and the accompanying spoken intents were also singular.

I wanted to make sure that my excitement and enthusiasm came across when I spoke about the work, so I asked myself why the technique that excited me so much. I decided that the most exciting aspect was being able to work in this new way on a newly accessible part of my being - the part of my being that held the key to my potential. I loved the fact that this work would lovingly empower me to move to the next step in my evolution and that working with others would lovingly empower them to do the same. This work was about empowerment, evolution and love. It represented the next step for humanity. All these things excited me.

Having thought about it all, I wrote down word for word my own explanation of the technique, of the UCL and an outline of the different sessions. Once I had done this, I felt more confident. Now I was really ready to start offering professional sessions.

The Word Spreads

Michael and I decided to work by word of mouth and so there was no need to prepare leaflets, but we did put posters of the UCL up in our house. At that time, Michael was teaching regular Reiki workshops and we had a steady stream of Reiki clients and students coming through our home.

Around a month or so after practitioner training, a regular Reiki client noticed the poster of the UCL and asked about it. After hearing our introduction, she decided to try an EMF Balancing Technique session. And so we gave our first professional session to our first client! From that day onwards we were never short of clients. More and more people came to us for sessions through various surprising avenues. It was quite amazing to witness.

Often a client would come to us for a Reiki session and decide to try out the EMF after noticing the poster and hearing about the work. Sometimes people we knew would ask us if we were doing anything new. People coming along to Reiki practice groups would sometimes express an interest in the poster on the wall and decide to have sessions. Other times people on Reiki workshops would ask me what else I did and many of those people became clients. One day Michael went out to post a letter and came back home with a client! He had bumped into someone he knew who was feeling very depressed and after hearing about EMF, she had decided to have a session immediately. Many of these people had very positive results from their sessions and they began to spread the word about the work to their family and friends, who then also came along to us for sessions. Word of mouth was beginning to work.

During this time Michael and I never attempted to persuade anyone to have sessions. We only told people about the work if they expressed an interest and we always empowered them to choose for themselves. In our mind there was no competition between The EMF Balancing Technique and Reiki. Both were very different and both had their unique worth. We always allowed people to decide what to have according to what felt right for them.

Other Avenues

One day we decided to contact a few friends and invite them to a free information evening about the new work we were doing. Using the notes I had prepared as a guide, I gave a talk about the work to around six people and then offered them free Mini Sessions. The evening was a great success and almost everyone booked in for sessions. One attendee loved it so much that she immediately booked onto the practitioner training.

Michael and I had added our names to the worldwide EMF website and every now and again someone would find us there and book in for sessions. People started to come to us from all kinds of sources. Some people had friends and family in other parts of the world who had had sessions in their own country and had recommended it to them. Michael and I loved it when clients came to us in this way as it reminded us that we were part of a worldwide community of practitioners working together co-operatively.

Over the next five or so months we gave over fifty sessions. Most people opted to have all the four phases available at the time so we got plenty of practice.

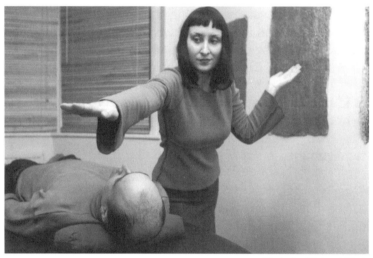

Photo by Richard Clark

Being an EMF Balancing Technique Practitioner

Overcoming My Fears

Being a professional practitioner was a big step forward for me personally and at first I was very apprehensive. I felt like a novice. Did I look like an EMF Balancing Technique practitioner? Was I really capable of doing this? I worried about making mistakes and not being able to answer people's questions. Lots of self doubts appeared. Would people trust me? What if something happened that I couldn't handle? What if I got difficult people? I kept reminding myself that I had carefully studied this work and I regularly took out my notes and reread them to revise the material. This gave me more confidence and I realised that the only way to conquer the fear was simply to give a session by myself to the best of my ability. So that's what I did.

My first session went very well. The client seemed happy with my explanation, enjoyed the session and even booked in for the next one! Once my first session was over, I felt much more relaxed. From then onwards I always attracted very pleasant clients who gave me very positive feedback and no situation ever arose that I could not handle. I took confidence in the fact that I was the EMF expert to my client, no matter how inexperienced I felt. After a while I understood that it was my own inner wisdom that was guiding this process for my highest good - just as in the sessions, the whole process of being a practitioner was self-regulating and self-directing. This knowledge made me feel secure and I began to trust myself.

Feeling the Energy of Love

From the very first session, being an EMF Balancing Technique practitioner was a completely amazing experience. Each time I said the opening words at the start of a session, I immediately felt the energy of pure love pour in. I felt it as a pressure in my whole body. My heart felt as if it was breaking and opening up. It was so overwhelming and intense that sometimes I could hardly breathe. Many times I would give breathless sessions with tears of joy streaming down my face. With each session, this energy intensified. However, in time I became accustomed to the sensations and emotions and I relaxed more and allowed the energy to bathe me and my client.

Sacred Work

Each and every session was a sacred experience. Moving my hands through each person's lattice and touching the fine strands was magical. At first I wanted to gasp out loud! I felt truly honoured to be working with people on this level. I felt at peace, strong and glowing during and after sessions. I continued to feel the energy of love strongly in every fibre of my being and it was truly exquisite. It was not just a concept - for me it began to be tangible, a reality that I could experience. I was beginning to understand what Peggy meant when she said that this technique was a delivery system for the energy of love.

Sacred Human

Giving sessions enabled me to truly appreciate the sacredness of each human being I came into contact with. I was aware of the support of the company we kept, but it was obvious to me that my client and I were doing the work ourselves, human to human. I felt that this work honoured the importance and wonder of being human and I was grateful for that.

Sacred Space

As soon as each session began, the front room of my house was transformed into the most wondrous sacred space and clients began to comment on this. This opened my eyes to the fact that sacredness is all around us in our everyday life - sacred space is everywhere. I could take this work anywhere and together my client and I would create our own space. From then onwards I gave the intent to see the sacredness in everything - in the people I met, in the things I said and in the things I did. I discovered a new reverence for my life and for life itself and I began to treat all with the greatest respect.

Working with the lattice was not only wondrous, it was also fun. I enjoyed performing the graceful movements and sensing the different parts of the lattice as I worked through it. I felt fulfilled. This was the best job I had ever had.

New Energies

Working with the UCL was very different to anything else I had experienced before and as I worked with the energies, I also noticed how unique they were too. They felt very subtle and gentle, yet also very tangible and potent. As new vibrations, they worked in a different way. When clients experienced releases of energy, they did not go through intense emotional catharsis - the energy enabled them to let go with balance and grace. People felt stronger in themselves and much more grounded after sessions. I became very familiar with these new energies - I could sense them and understand their qualities and characteristics. As I continued to give sessions, witness the outcomes and note the feedback, I kept learning more and more about these energies, the UCL and the EMF Balancing Technique.

Client Feedback

One of our very first clients was a man in his seventies, a retired electrical engineer, who had come on the recommendation of his daughter. He was completely new to energy work - yet something about the work attracted him. During his sessions he felt absolutely nothing but he did tell us that despite having been an insomniac for some years, he had actually slept for some hours after the first session. Also, at the end of every session he said he felt very relaxed. Sometimes other clients came along who also did not feel the energy at all, but they all reported feelings of relaxation and stillness. With relief, I realised that the sessions worked regardless of whether people felt the energy.

Joy

Whilst some people told us that they felt calm and peaceful, others were very joyful and couldn't stop laughing. Some even felt ecstatic and were moved to tears, describing the feeling as one of 'bliss'. Many clients commented on how safe and nurtured they felt during the sessions, almost like being cocooned in gentle and soothing energy.

Feeling and Seeing the Energy

Many clients felt the energy very tangibly and reported various sensations such as tingling, static, electricity, warmth, heat and ice cold. Feeling pulling or tugging sensations was also very common. Some people saw very clear images of different parts of their UCL in their mind's eye. Others experienced intuitive flashes and vivid dream-like sequences.

Fully Present in their Body

Clients would very often stand up at the end of their session and tell me that they felt much more present in their body, more grounded and more solid. One client said that she experienced coming into her body for the first time ever and another told me that her body now felt like a sacred place to be in. I met many people who told me that they had always felt disconnected from their body and had never been fully present before, yet after the sessions they finally experienced being comfortable with their body and began to feel at home.

Feeling 'Different'

Many people said that after the sessions they felt somehow 'different', but they couldn't quite put their finger on exactly what it was that had changed. Some felt more confident and stronger in themselves. Others were more specific about how differently they suddenly felt about their life and themselves. One lady said that for the first time in her life she was starting to feel that she too deserved to have all the things that she saw others had - her self worth was returning. Another lady, who had been feeling depressed and lethargic, came off the treatment couch with renewed vigour for life, having ideas about new things that she could learn and do. She was much more optimistic and positive. One client emailed me later to say that she now felt the time had come to move on with her life, which was very liberating for her.

Each Session was Unique

I was incredibly happy and honoured to be able to help people in this way. It was very interesting to see how everyone had their own unique experience of each session, yet at the same time reported similar experiences to others in their feedback. The work was interesting and intrigued me. Although I performed exactly the same movements and repeated the same words each time, every session was unique and the feedback I got from clients was always uplifting, sometimes even amazing.

I noticed that sometimes the benefits were physical as well as emotional. One lady who had suffered from heart palpitations for months found that they had gone immediately after receiving her session. Another client had been depressed for a long time, yet after his sessions he told me that the depression had lifted and he felt 'normal' again. Many clients said that they felt so much clearer headed, as if a fog had lifted and fewer thoughts were running around their heads. One client described this as feeling less of a tension between his self and his intellect.

Non-Cathartic

I first witnessed the unique qualities of this work with a long-term regular Reiki client. This client had always had very intense emotional and physical reactions to his Reiki, both during and after the sessions. When he expressed an interest in the EMF Balancing Technique, I was delighted and also curious to see what would happen. As we began the first session, he started to react in his usual extreme way. However, within minutes this began to lessen and I watched, fascinated and somewhat amused, as the cathartic response gradually lessened and eventually disappeared, so that by the end of the session he was completely peaceful and still. When he came for the next session, his usual response did not even begin and from then onwards he never reacted in his old way again. The contrast was so extreme that it was almost comical and I had to stop myself laughing aloud. I began to think that here was someone who was maybe somehow addicted to this kind of reaction, who was expecting himself to behave in this way. Yet now this energy just didn't encompass or encourage that kind of reaction. At the end of every session he told me that he felt much more balanced and, most importantly, 'more himself'. This process was very different and much more gentle than anything else he had experienced before, he said. Witnessing these sessions was proof to me that this work really did enable people to release and transform without a deeply cathartic response.

From then onwards, I began to get feedback which constantly reaffirmed this idea. People told me that they had chosen this work precisely because of its gentle non-cathartic aspect. They could feel that this was a different way of working and no longer wanted to suffer in order to release old patterns. It was a welcome relief for many.

Moving On

As I gave more and more sessions, I noticed how the work helped people to move forwards by allowing them to let go of the old patterns holding them back. One lady, who had felt stuck in her past for a very long time, came for some sessions. Having had them, she then went back to see her usual practitioner of another modality. This practitioner was amazed by the transformation in her and said that she seemed to have let go and become more open to change. She finally felt free, as if the old binds had been loosened and she could now begin to move on.

Many clients told me that the sessions helped them to feel more detached from their past. Old issues and challenges no longer had a hold over them. Although they were still aware of past events, they now felt more objective about them, more able to cope and move forward. This made them feel lighter and also helped them to feel differently about their future. They now felt confident that they could actually make things happen!

All this feedback was exciting as it confirmed over and over again just how different working with the UCL is. I witnessed the new energy dynamics in action - in the new paradigm personal growth can be done with balance and grace, without suffering and catharsis.

Tact and Gentleness

From time to time, clients would ask me if I could see their lattice and analyse it for them, particularly if they had long held issues they were intent on releasing. Even though my intuition was heightening by the day, I always reflected the question back, asking them what they themselves had experienced during their session. It was not important for me to know what energetic shifts had occurred in the session and it was never my focus to find out. I knew that the aim of the work was to help people to get in touch with their UCL in their own unique way. I hoped to encourage people to begin to trust their inner wisdom and sense their own energy. I knew that this would lead to greater self trust and was infinitely more empowering than relying on the practitioner for diagnosis. I knew that I was not fixing anything, I was merely following a series of movements to which each client's inner wisdom would respond. There was no need for me to even know what the client wanted to release - work could be done on a deep level whilst respecting the client's privacy. Having always tried to be tactful and gentle with people in my life, I was very happy with this approach as I felt it was non-invasive and respected each person's private space. This was what being in service in the new energy dynamics really meant. It just allowed people to be. To me it was a real honouring of who that person was without any need to interfere.

The Client's Inner Wisdom

Over those months I witnessed a wide range of responses to the sessions. I saw for myself how this energy was self regulating and self-directing. I was giving every client exactly the same session, yet each response was unique. Their inner wisdom was determining what they needed at that time - it had nothing to do with me and it felt good to be giving the power back to the client. I was always aware that I was a facilitator, and that the sessions helped the person to come into balance and bring them greater well-being in their own personal way. The wide range of responses showed me that well-being could sometimes but not always entail physical healing. At times it seemed as if healing in the way that we had always defined it did not take place, yet the client achieved greater inner peace in spite of this. I began to redefine my own idea of 'healing' over time and I realised that it was a multifaceted concept. 'Healing' could mean physical, emotional, mental or spiritual benefits - each person's inner wisdom would always decide.

I loved the universality of the work - people of all different backgrounds, ages and belief systems came for sessions. I had always been a passionate believer in equality and this work represented that for me. Everyone had a UCL, no matter what their background, and everyone received the same session.

My Experience Grew

Every session I gave provided me with deeper insights into the energy. During those few months I built up a large amount of experience. With every session I did, I learnt a little more as each client told me something unique. I kept records of every session and took note of what every client told me. I remembered each person's feedback and would often think about their experience, connecting it to what I was reading, studying and experiencing within myself. This was the work in action, not just in theory. After a while, I found that similar experiences and questions would arise and when they did, I could answer and give advice. And so my experience as a practitioner grew.

Later on, as my confidence and knowledge grew, experienced energy workers came along for sessions. They had more demanding questions, but I was always able to answer them. Even though they had many more years experience of energy work than me, the EMF Balancing Technique worked in a very different way to other modalities and I now had plenty of experience with it. I always felt very energised after each session, never drained, as there had been no exchange of personal energy between me and my client. I started to feel the benefits for myself as well. Things happened for me in my life after each session, and I learnt from each situation and so progressed in my wisdom and understanding. I felt comfortable being an EMF Balancing Technique practitioner and it felt good to witness positive changes in other people. I had finally found work that excited and inspired me!

Integrity and Empowerment

Having sensed the integrity of the way Peggy and Steve Dubro worked, Michael and I intended to do the same and honour their work. Right from the very start we always aimed to empower and respect our clients. We tried to keep the integrity of the work intact, behave lovingly to others and work co-operatively with other practitioners and teachers.

One aspect of this involved empowering clients to decide when to come back for their next session. Some clients decided to come back right away the next day while others preferred to wait a little longer. We never advised or decided for them. I felt strongly that stepping back and encouraging others to trust their own intuition was all part of being a practitioner in this new paradigm.

Co-operation and Non-Competition

Working co-operatively was particularly important to us. Whenever someone contacted us for a session, we checked to see if there were other practitioners near to them and then let people choose which practitioner they preferred. We knew that clients would always choose the appropriate practitioner for them, according to their inner wisdom and we did not want to interfere with that process. We also knew that there would always be plenty of clients to go round, so there was no need to fear not having enough. In our minds there was no competition between us and other practitioners - we were all in this together! We found that co-operating with other practitioners and empowering clients in this way aligned us with the energy of the work and our practice thrived. We also regularly used the tools for co-creating that we had learnt on the practitioner training course. Consequently we were never short of clients.

Respect for Other Modalities

As well as respecting our clients and other practitioners, Michael and I also aimed to respect other modalities. We knew that just as there is no competition between EMF practitioners, so there exists none between complementary modalities. Believing that all modalities have their worth and there is space for everyone, we never judged the EMF Balancing Technique against other work. Sending out this message of co-operation to the universe reflected back into our personal lives and we found that events generally flowed very smoothly for us and we experienced little conflict.

Following the Set Pattern

I had decided on the practitioner training course to faithfully follow the set pattern of movements for each session. And performing the same movements and saying the same words each time suited me very well. Not being an experienced energy worker, I found that having a structure to work with enabled me to learn the technique more quickly and helped me to build up my confidence as a practitioner. It was also very liberating as there was no pressure to feel, analyse, predict, diagnose or intuit and I was able to focus on practising the movements and gain my own experience of the energy. I found that each time I spoke the say alouds, I would reach a deeper understanding of the words and they often related to things that were happening to me personally in my own life. I knew that the good feedback I was getting from my clients was due to my fidelity to the technique's structure. It was the reason why they felt in such a safe and nurturing space and more balanced when releasing. I was happy in the knowledge that I was doing this work as Peggy desired.

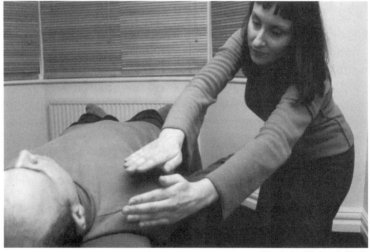

Photo by Richard Clark

Personal Growth

Privileged

When I thought about all the profound knowledge about myself I had been given on the workshop, I felt so privileged and blessed that I was determined not to let it go to waste. I owed it to myself and to others in my life. I felt truly fortunate to be alive during these exciting times and I was grateful to all the others before me who had worked so hard to create the new paradigm.

Practice! Practice! Practice!

During those first few months Peggy's words resounded in my head, "Practice, practice, practice!" and I understood the importance of them. With the same commitment and perseverance a martial artist dedicates to his art, I dedicated myself to the work. I gave sessions, I chose a meditation to do every day, I actively used my UCL and I revised the material from the course. And I often thought about the work and how it affected my life. My aim was to achieve inner peace, abundance, wisdom, love and balance. But I knew that achieving these things required some time and effort on my part, so I kept on focusing. Most of all, I committed myself to living the principles of pure intent, integrity, love and compassion in my daily life. I wanted to walk my talk. It was not always easy and I slipped up a few times along the way, but in time, I could see that my goal was coming nearer and nearer. It was working, so I kept on going. The workshop had introduced me to the work, now it was time for me to make it happen.

And things certainly happened! I moved onto a rapid learning curve. Until then the energy of love, pure intent and empowerment had been concepts, but I was to learn what it meant to experience them in my daily life in a very real way.

Self Worth

I learned many lessons and the first was how to say no to things that were inappropriate or unhealthy for me. I attracted people and situations into my life where my boundaries were pushed to the limit. This obliged me to say "no more!" and redefine my limits. I began to ask myself questions such as "How do I want to spend my time and who do I want to spend it with?", "What am I prepared to tolerate?", "Who and what do I want to give my energy to?". I knew that this was the first step towards empowerment and increased self worth. I had to learn to be clear about what I felt and to express that to others in a gentle and loving way. I rethought many of my values, and as a result I learned to respect myself more. From the experiences I had with others, I became much more aware in general and learned how to spot an unhealthy situation and make the necessary changes. My life became much simpler.

Who I Really Am

I found that people began to challenge me on what I believed in and how I worked and lived my life. After a while I realised that these were questions I needed to clarify within myself. Once I had defined exactly who I was to myself, I began to feel stronger and more confident. I found that the EMF work had provided me with a language for expressing ideas and ways of being that had always been instinctive to me - I had just never had the words to express them. The say alouds from the sessions were actually helping me to speak up in my daily life. Being shy about speaking the say alouds as a practitioner reflected my shyness in my life with others. The more I practised both, the easier it all became. After so long, I refound my voice. However, the challenges did not disappear, as I had expected! They sometimes reemerged with different questions, and knowing that this was going to be a constant process, I learned to see them as opportunities to learn about myself and to grow.

In time I was grateful for them as they helped me to become more and more of who I really was. Using the tools I had learnt on practitioner training proved invaluable during this time. They helped me to release and rebalance as I learnt and grew.

Self Responsibility

I knew that the energy in my UCL was creating the people, things and events in my life and I knew exactly how this was happening. The experiences I was attracting were encouraging me to take more responsibility for my own life and I was happy to do this. As I noted what was happening and took steps to change what I was not happy with using my EMF tools, I began to feel more and more empowered. I understood that accepting greater responsibility was all part of having more control over my own life, and it felt good. I constantly reminded myself of my own accumulated wisdom held in the back of my UCL. I knew that I could draw upon it to help me in my life right now, and this gave me a feeling of being supported, especially during challenging moments. I focused on the back fibres of my UCL often, familiarising myself with them. And by doing this I found much comfort and strength from within.

Growing Without Suffering

As a result of all the energetic work I was doing and my continued focus, I let go of much old energy during those first few months. I could sense that my UCL was constantly recalibrating to the next level. And what I noted in my own life was similar to what my clients were telling me. Releasing old energy was not deeply cathartic or traumatic. In fact, much of the time the process seemed to be gentle, especially when I used the sessions and say alouds to help me along. For a while I did experience a feeling of emptiness, despite being contented with my life. It felt as if I was mourning someone close to me who had died but I tried not to dwell on this feeling. I kept reminding myself that I had to empty out before I could fill up again, that this was a part of the transformation process of me becoming more and more of who I really was and who I wanted to be. I knew that this deep transformation could not take place overnight and by being patient with myself and accepting the process, gradually the emptiness subsided. Bit by bit, I began to feel fuller. Having shared much of my life with a feeling of emptiness, this incredible new sense of well-being and joy that I was feeling was just amazing. It felt as though I had shed the old me and been reborn.

Spiralling Into My Potential

Having been reborn, I could sense myself beginning to spiral into my potential. Being an EMF Balancing Technique practitioner, I began to discover what I was capable of. I regularly gave myself the sessions which focused on activating my hidden talents and latent abilities and removing any fears and worries about moving forward. And I continued to use the front of my UCL to plant seeds of the potentials I desired for my life. This process worked, for over time, more and more aspects of myself opened up. I was able to confidently talk to people about this work, I found I was perfectly capable of being a practitioner and I was finally able to stand up for the things I believed in and start living the life I had always dreamed of. There was obviously a lot more to me than met the eye! The more I did the work, the happier I became and the process of self discovery continued.

Taking Part

With this work I began to move forward in my life. I was actively taking part and helping people, spreading this wonderful energy of empowerment. I was doing, not just being. I felt as if I was finally here and being heard, doing my bit, helping the world. I often thought back with nostalgia to the year before and those intense months I had spent alone in my flat. The experiences of energy were now being replaced with a new sense of who I was. It was also replaced with happiness that I was taking an active part and new insights and experiences with the UCL and the EMF Balancing Technique. I did not miss my previous experiences, but neither did I dismiss them. They had been an integral part of my awakening and had taught me a lot. But now I had a new part of the energy field to explore and I had an exciting new energy to work with. I was moving into a new level of understanding.

What became important to me was telling people about this new part of themselves which contributed so greatly to their empowerment. It could help them create the potentials they desired in their lives, find more inner peace, connect more deeply with their inner knowing and take control of their lives. In the few months since practitioner training, my focus had shifted. I wanted to help people feel more grounded, more here and ready to play their own particular part in life on earth.

My Body

Being aware of my UCL and using it in my life, I noticed my relationship with my body changing. I gradually became more aware of the importance of looking after it - I began to exercise more and eat healthier food. I began to listen to my body and respect it as a part of my being that I could not separate from the rest of me. Over time I felt happier and happier with my body. This was a new experience for me for I had spent much of my life dealing with physical ailments and tortured by my unhappiness with my physical appearance. I also began to feel much more present, alive and really here on earth. The years of not wanting to be here, always being on the run, feeling neither settled nor at home, were over. Looking back, I knew that I had been 'out of my body' but now I was happy to be here. I was finally able to say this with confidence.

A Balanced Relationship

Now that the universe was well and truly aware of my unique presence, I set about ensuring that the relationship between us was balanced. I began to focus regularly on the side fibres of my UCL, which contained the energy of my giving and receiving. Having assessed both, I firstly called back any energy I was sending out that seemed unhealthy, draining or that I felt was more worthwhile to me elsewhere. I then gave the intent to be open to be able to receive more. And finally I gave the intent for the energy I was giving out on my right to be in balance with the energy I was receiving on my left. When I did this exercise, I would immediately feel more balanced and more in the flow. By doing this I was changing the message I was giving out to the universe and telling it that I wanted to be in a balanced partnership, so the universe could respond to me in a more balanced way. I realised that it was up to me to do this. The universe would only reflect back to me the message I gave out. I did this regularly and, as a result, my life changed.

The Next Step

Since practitioner training, I had witnessed many positive changes within myself and my clients. I realised just how amazing this technique really was - I had seen it work over and over again. I had seen people brighten up and let go of old patterns with much more grace and ease than I had thought possible. I decided that I wanted to take it a step further. I wanted to be able to spread the word and reach more people, and I felt strongly that becoming a teacher would help me do this. Michael and I checked Peggy's schedule on the worldwide website - she was going to teach a teacher training in Belgium in October. We booked on.

A Wonderful Offer

Catching up with a good friend one evening, I mentioned this latest development in my life. My friend Hilary is an editor and at that time was working for the London Metro, a free national daily newspaper with a distribution of around a million. Hilary said that she would first have to check with her editor, but she was interested in writing an article about EMF for the Metro. It was a very casual conversation and although I was happy about her offer, I soon forgot about it.

Placing Our Trust

As we were taking our next step with the work, we decided to dedicate our whole space to our work and so just before we left for Belgium to do the teacher training, our lodger left. We were aware that from then onwards on we would have to pay all the rent and the bills for the house ourselves and we were going to support ourselves by doing this work full time. It seemed a daunting step to take but we knew it was the right thing for us. We were stepping out together and it involved placing our total trust in the process. But trusting was something I had become very good at over the last year or so. I had placed myself in the care of the universe and I had always been looked after - no harm had ever come to me, and I knew that absolute trust and dedication were always rewarded.

Nerves

As teacher training loomed, my usual fears resurfaced. What was I doing? Was I really capable of teaching this? Wasn't I too new to energy work, too much of a novice? I needed some confirmation! It came. A week or so before we were due to leave for Belgium Greig and Lorianne, back from their European trip, suddenly got in touch with us again. I told them that we were soon going to train to become EMF teachers but that my insecurities were coming up and it all seemed too daunting for me. "Lina", said Lorianne gently, "You are a teacher." That was all I needed to hear.

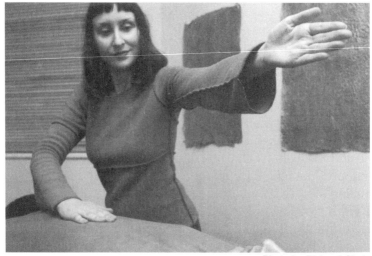

Photo by Richard Clark

Acceleration

And So It Began!

Teacher Training

Driving to Belgium for teacher training was so exciting that I soon forgot all about my nervousness and as the days went by, I began to feel that I really *could* do this. Each day we were specially trained in how to prepare ourselves energetically for a class. When we did these exercises, I began to feel that I really was an EMF Balancing Technique teacher. I could sense that my energy was readjusting itself to help me feel comfortable with being a teacher. The training also provided us with plenty of practical materials to use in class. At the end of the training Michael and I approached Peggy to say goodbye. Her final words to us that day were "Now go out there and teach!" I was ready to do that now and I was going to take Peggy at her word!

Revision

Once at home, I took out all my materials: the notes I had made on the training, Michael's notes, my teacher manual and my workbooks. I read and absorbed every single word. I needed to make sure that I understood this before I could teach it. I was organising myself mentally to make sure it all made sense.

Metro Article

A few days later, my friend Hilary contacted me again. She had checked with her editor, she said, and he was happy for her to write an article about the EMF Balancing Technique. Amidst all the excitement and preparation, I had forgotten all about her offer. We decided that the best way to go about it would be to give Hilary the four phases and invite her to an information evening so that she could learn more about the work. Hilary enjoyed the sessions and found that afterwards, some positive changes happened in her life. She wrote her article and sent along a photographer to take some pictures of us for her piece. However, to our disappointment, the article was delayed for a couple of months. Each time it was due to be published, another bigger news story would override it at the last moment. In the end, Michael and I decided to put thoughts about the article to one side. We both agreed that if the article was meant to be, it would happen at the perfect time for us. During that time, we began to receive enquiries and bookings and by the end of the year we had taught a few people the Basic Training, including Jackie Calderwood, the friend who had been with Michael the day he had met Greig and Lorianne and who later went on to become a teacher herself.

One evening in early January 2001, Hilary suddenly called. Her article was definitely going to be in tomorrow morning's paper, she told us. As soon as I heard, I gave the intent that everybody who resonated with this work would be attracted to the article. Michael and I were both incredibly excited and decided to get up extra early the next morning and head down to the nearest tube station to grab a few copies before they all went! That evening we put together some information to give to people and we set a few dates for information evenings. We both agreed that an information evening was a great way for people to find out about the work, plus they could meet us and get a free Mini Session to experience the energy too.

It was still dark and quiet outside as we made our way to the tube station early the next morning. When we reached the station we ran towards the newspaper stall and grabbed a few copies of the Metro. I hurriedly opened one of the papers - and amazingly I opened it right at the very page the article was on! We scanned it quickly - it looked great. On our way back home, we decided not to have too many expectations and reasoned that even if only a handful of people called, that would be fine by us. But as soon as we got back to our front door we could hear the phone ringing, and we rushed inside to answer it. It was our first enquiry! It was the first of many. Throughout that day we received over fifty calls. Michael was teaching and so I answered the phone, taking people's details and booking them into one of our information evenings. Whilst Michael was on breaks he took over phone duty for me so that I could eat and get dressed! At the end of his teaching day Michael mailed or emailed our information to everyone who had enquired. People continued to call until the evening. The next day the calls continued, but this time there were two of us and we had a system in place. I answered the calls, relayed the information simultaneously to Michael who then immediately emailed the information to the caller. Over those two days we received around a hundred calls and we managed to get back to everyone in forty eight hours!

Knowing that in a few days up to ten people were going to be sitting in my house listening to me speaking about the work, I polished my information evening notes and waited for the adventure to begin!

Being an EMF Balancing Technique Teacher

Information Evenings

People began to turn up. Each evening I was terribly nervous but each evening I kept surprising myself by talking to complete strangers with some level of authority and confidence. Once I started, I found that talking about the EMF Balancing Technique came naturally to me. I was speaking from my heart about something that I loved and that had helped me so much in my life. Also, my experience as a practitioner proved to be invaluable as I was able to draw on client feedback and the results I had witnessed. Some evenings went more smoothly than others and I witnessed many different reactions to the information. I spoke to all kinds of people - some experienced energy workers, some completely new to energy work, some open, some sceptical, some deliberately antagonistic, some overjoyed to be hearing this information at last. I encountered many people who thought very differently about energy, who worked in very different ways and were very vocal about this. But they did not throw me. I used the special energy exercise from the teacher training and this enabled me to stay focused and balanced throughout so that I could handle all the different types of people and questions that arose. I knew that this technique works in a very unique way, so I did not worry.

Aware that I was actually attracting these people myself with my own energy, I gradually became more detached and stronger within myself. Each person - whether open or sceptical - taught me something about myself, about human nature and energy. I passionately believed in the work and my enthusiasm carried me through. I focused on the good feedback and became more and more confident talking to strangers about the EMF Balancing Technique. Mostly people were very receptive and some started to book onto our workshops. My voice was becoming stronger too. I had already learnt so much and come so far, I thought. But as soon as I began teaching, I realised that the learning curve became steeper. This was to be serious growth.

The Adventure Begins

Michael and I began to teach small classes in the front room of our house. As there wasn't enough space for a large table in that room, we had decided to buy large beanbags for people to sit on. We found that this arrangement suited us really well - the atmosphere was informal and the small groups meant that we could give people more personal attention and check movements more carefully. It was the perfect environment for us and it suited our teaching style. The smaller groups also meant that we were broken in gently. We were in a familiar place and everything we needed was to hand. Each month between two to six people turned up for the training. Now and again a seventh person would enquire and Michael and I would hurriedly search for another venue. But funnily enough, that seventh person would always cancel at the last minute, leaving us with our comfortable home set-up. We took this to mean that this was the most appropriate way to work and we were both more than happy with this.

Teaching turned out to be much easier than I had expected. Just before each class I did the special energy exercise. Amazingly, even though I felt afraid and nervous, this exercise would immediately put me into a very special posture - I would feel strong and confident and very much connected to the work. Any nerves would just evaporate and this state would last all day. Once I started talking, I was carried along by the momentum of the class and the energy and then the workshops flowed smoothly. I found that I understood things at just the right moment and the right words came when I needed them. If there was something I wasn't quite sure about, I double checked it with Peggy later.

Michael and I taught classes every month, even if it was for just one person. We found that every month was different and people seemed to turn up in waves. Because of this continuity I became more and more familiar with the information and over time my teaching became clearer and more concise. We experimented a little - sometimes I would teach the morning session whilst Michael supported and Michael would teach the afternoon while I supported. After a while we would swap and in this way we both gained experience of teaching different parts of the workshop. The notion that I was a novice when it came to energy work soon wore off when I found myself answering questions with ease. Over time I felt more authoritative in my role as an EMF Balancing Technique teacher.

Being the Best Representative I Can Be

I wanted to be the best representative of the work that I could possibly be and for me one aspect of this was to teach the technique to people exactly as I had been taught by Peggy herself. I impressed upon every practitioner the importance of performing the movements as precisely as possible and following the set pattern. This means never omitting or adding anything and never breaking off to do something else. The importance of this was shown to me again and again for every month I had ample opportunities of witnessing first hand how much difference a slight adjustment or a small refinement of a movement makes. I realised that by teaching people so precisely, I was ensuring that I was passing on the technique in its purest form, which meant that anyone could learn to do this. All people had to do was follow the technique as they had been taught in class and they would be able to instantly give wonderful and effective sessions.

Also, with delight, I saw that this was indeed a repeatable system. I was passing on the technique to others myself in the same way that Peggy had passed it on to me! The form was allowing us to spread the teachings and the energy effectively.

Deliberate to Automatic

Teaching became easier and easier with time. As I became more familiar with the material, my words and explanations flowed more smoothly. My delivery moved from deliberate to automatic. But despite repeating the same information every month, it was never boring. Every class was completely different. Each time people asked different questions, giving me more to think about and leading me to a deeper understanding of the work. I was constantly being prompted to think about the work in a whole new way.

Joy

The work was very joyful to teach. Every time I noticed how empowering and uplifting people found the information. I could see them brightening up as they went through the training. Being able to share such enlightening information with people was so wonderful. Watching them transform was amazing and I was so grateful to be able to do this for a living.

Not everyone who came along for information evenings trained with us. Many people chose to have sessions instead. Our front room doubled up as a session room, but because of the sheer volume of demand, this was just not enough. So Michael and I converted a bedroom upstairs into a temporary session room and whilst Michael gave sessions downstairs, I gave sessions upstairs. It was a very busy year - we worked non-stop, teaching workshops once a month, running weekly information evenings and giving a steady stream of sessions.

Giving regular sessions was great. Not only was I able to help people and keep my own energy balanced, it was also a great complement to my teaching. The sessions provided me with excellent experiences I could draw upon as real life examples during the training. It was enriching my workshops. My learning was accelerated and constant.

A Teacher Teaches What They Need to Learn

Being a teacher had a profound effect upon my personal life, which in turn profoundly affected my workshops. Every month I delivered the same information, happy to be teaching concepts I passionately believed in myself. After a while, though, I noticed an intriguing process was unfolding in my life. Between workshops, particular experiences would happen in my life which highlighted particular concepts I taught on the workshops. People, events and situations arose, bringing me face to face with spiritual truths and obliging me to work through and learn from them. Each time was different. For a while I noticed that I was attracting sceptical and judgemental people who challenged me and made me feel angry and upset. I found myself falling into blame and judgement. Then I remembered Peggy saying that she sees the face of God in everyone and I realised that practising this would be beneficial for me too! So I made a great effort to stay in my Core in these situations, remain compassionate and look to other people's Core Energy. This helped me to stay sensitive while developing resilience and the challenging situations gradually stopped.

On my next workshop I was able to speak about Core Energy and what this meant with added depth from personal experience. The concept had come alive for me. This amazing process continued. Opportunities to learn came regularly and each time I applied my EMF techniques and understanding, which moved me quickly along a path of self-discovery and wisdom. I was finding out exactly what certain concepts actually felt like in real life - what they really meant for people in every day life and it was making me a 'better' teacher.

UK Co-ordinators

Very soon after the article was published in the Metro, Peggy and Steve invited us to take on the role of UK co-ordinators for the technique. We were honoured to be asked and accepted the role very happily. I felt my connection to the work deepen and having taken on my new role, I stepped up my intention to align with the energy even more in my professional capacity. Having come face to face with what I was teaching in my own life, I knew that it was important for me to embody what I was teaching. I gave intent to do that.

Non-Competition

Michael and I had always worked co-operatively and we intended to continue in this way. Believing that co-operation is the essence of the EMF work, as teachers and co-ordinators we aimed to encourage other teachers and practitioners to work together. After working mainly through word of mouth for nearly two years and never having been short of work, we totally believed that there are always enough students and clients for every teacher and practitioner. We took it upon ourselves to be open and truthful with enquirers, recommending other teachers nearer to them. We knew that there is no such thing as anyone's 'territory' or anyone's students - teachers and students find each other for many reasons. Intuitively, we knew that the energy flowed of its own accord, in its self-regulating and self-directing way and we did not want to impede that flow.

Every time we recommended a student to a teacher nearer to them, we received something back from the universe. It did sometimes take a conscious effort to do this and one month in particular was an enormous learning experience for us. That month, our finances were a little tight and we began to be a little concerned. It was a week before the workshop, and only one person had booked in for half the training. When we checked the UK teaching schedule, we saw that another teacher was running a workshop only a short distance from this person's home. Although we knew that this would leave us with nobody at all for the whole training, we also knew that it was the right thing to give her back her deposit and refer her to the other teacher and so, a little anxiously, we did. And then, miraculously, over the next few days leading up to the workshop, we got one booking after another, as if out of nowhere! That month turned out to be a very abundant one - we received five bookings, the students were wonderful and we all had a fun and enlightening week.

By being open and staying in our integrity, we were rewarded. By letting go of the fear of lack, the energy flowed more smoothly to us. We continue to hold this vision for everyone - all practitioners and teachers of the EMF Balancing Technique working together as a community, wherever they are in the world.

Integrity

Michael and I continued to roll up our sleeves and get on with the work, always in a respectful and honest way in keeping with its purity and integrity. We very much wanted to honour Peggy and Steve and their team for all the hard work we knew they constantly put into the EMF Balancing Technique. And we wanted to honour all other practitioners and teachers and encourage them to show a united front by acting as a community. This integrity and hard work has been rewarded with a flourishing practice, for which we are very grateful.

The Energy of Money

I knew that learning to be comfortable with the energy of money was a key concept in working in this new paradigm and as we became clearer about this, our business grew in strength. Michael and I always took advance deposits for our workshops and were very clear and open about the cost of them. I also knew that it was linked to my self worth - I deserved to be paid for all the time, money and effort I myself was putting into embodying and spreading this work. Money was an exchange of energy for all those things. And I deserved to be paid enough so that I could earn a living from doing what I loved.

Running an Ethical Business

Having decided to run an ethical business, we kept accurate accounts. This kept our financial exchange with the universe very clear and gradually we became more and more abundant. Only a few months earlier we had, with trepidation, given the intent to make a living from doing energy work with pure intent - and now it was really happening and it felt amazing. For me this was a dream come true. I was living the life I had always wanted, the life which had until then evaded me - the life of a contented, fulfilled person in a loving, stable relationship making a living doing something I loved.

Feedback

Very soon practitioners we had taught began to contact us with their feedback. They had had fun on the workshops. A couple of people referred to the training as one of the best experiences of their lives. Many people were excited about what they had learnt, particularly about moving to the next step in their evolution. What people loved about the work was that it helped them to feel more empowered and strengthened. It was also very practical and easy to use. People started to tell us that they had received pay rises or promotions at work and had generally became more abundant in their lives. After a while we saw that these were not coincidences, but a by-product of the increased self-worth and self-empowerment that the energetic changes on the workshop had produced in the practitioners. It was most heart-warming when people thanked us for helping them to change their lives and begin doing what they really love. Many people went on to become professional practitioners, earning money from the sessions they gave. I was thrilled to see that what had happened for me was actually happening for others too - confirmation again that this was indeed a repeatable system.

In the spring of 2002 Lorianne took the UCL workshop with me. It was an honour to share the information with one of the two people who had told me about the technique and helped me to change my life. That day was significant for me - I had a sense of coming full circle.

The Fast Lane

During 2001 I learnt much about working professionally in the field of energy work and all the experiences I had helped me to work with more integrity, love and wisdom. This growth was reflected in my personal life. Working with the EMF Balancing Technique helped me to become a wiser, more loving, peaceful and discerning person.

Loudspeaker on Full Blast

The UCL is our own personal connection to the Cosmic Lattice (the Universe) and when its energetic pathways are activated and balanced our thoughts, words, emotions and actions are transmitted much more loudly than ever before. And the consequences of those thoughts, words, emotions and actions come back to us more quickly than ever before. I remembered the analogy of the UCL being compared to having a loudspeaker added to your energy field. Being a teacher and working with the energy of this work made me realise that not only was there a loudspeaker in my energy field, it was also turned up full blast and transmitting at top volume!

Mirror

The high speed at which my UCL reflected back to me was astounding. Every day I experienced just how much my connection to the universe had deepened and just how personal that connection had become. It astonished me at first to see myself continuously reflected back to me in such stark clarity. All those years of running away from myself were over. With my UCL in place, the universe knew exactly who and where I was. I couldn't escape the mirror. This process helped me to become increasingly more self-aware. I was going to have to take even greater responsibility for everything I did, said, felt and thought. I noticed how any time I expressed negativity about something or someone, that same negativity came back to me very quickly. If I was judgmental about someone or something, then pretty soon afterwards a judgmental person would turn up in my life and be judgmental about me! I never got away with it! I realised just how linked everyone is - by saying hurtful things about someone else, I was really just hurting myself. My UCL helped me to focus on being in my integrity, not just in class but in every moment of my daily life.

The Power of Words

I saw how the power of my words had become particularly amplified and over time I became clearer and more gentle with my choice of them. It wasn't always so easy and naturally I slipped up at times, but my intent was to do it better the next time and I kept on focusing on this. I knew I wasn't perfect. I also knew that this process was not some rigorous test set up by a judgemental and harsh universe; the universe was not waiting for me to slip up in order to punish me. My own energy was merely reflecting back to me some things about myself that I could choose to work on, if I wished. If I chose to ignore them, they came back at another time, presenting me with another opportunity to work on them. It was always my choice. We are beings of free will and we are free to create what we choose.This was me talking to me! Knowing this enabled me to learn to stop judging myself so much whenever I felt that I hadn't acted in my integrity. I was practising my mastery and it would become easier the more I used it. After a while, seeing a part of myself I wasn't too keen on reflected back even became a little comical and I learned to smile about it.

Core Energy

Having been brought up in a very conditional, critical family, I constantly battled with being judgmental. Non-judgement was something I aspired to. As I watched Michael in his compassionate and tolerant dealings with others, I wished I could be more like him. As I worked towards my goal, my greatest tool became working with Core Energy.

Each time I found myself becoming judgmental towards someone, I immediately focused on their Core Energy and reminded myself what this energy represented. I visualised it running through their being, a column of pure bright light. However they were behaving at that moment was not who they really were, the Core Energy was who they really were, just as it was who I really was. I then activated and radiated my own Core Energy, as I had been taught and this helped me to connect with the nobler aspects of myself, rather than the judgmental part of myself. Doing this had a wonderful effect. Seeing someone with the eyes of my Core Energy helped me to become more compassionate and patient with people.

The more I did this, the easier it became. It had a knock-on effect onto the rest of my life too and I noticed my relationships with others changing. My family started to become more open and communicative with me. Although it was not glaringly obvious, I sensed that my father was softening towards me. He was still distant, but he was now and again taking a little time to talk to me. It was a subtle difference, but one I appreciated. This was powerful evidence to me that once you change the energy inside yourself, your relationships and your life change along with you. You truly do create your own reality from the inside out!

More Resilient

Radiating my Core Energy helped me in many ways. Over the years, people had often accused me of being 'too sensitive' and it was the bane of my life. I had always felt everything and everyone around me so deeply. I was easily and profoundly affected by other people's feelings, thoughts and energy and this heightened the more I worked with energy. Working with my Core Energy helped me to become stronger as I radiated outwards. The more I did this, the more resilient I felt. I continued to feel deeply, yet I noticed that I was gradually becoming more able to be detached. Having such an effective tool enabled me to begin to see my sensitivity as a gift, not a drawback and this made a difference for I noticed that people stopped commenting on it!

The Answers Within Me

I used my Core Energy often and particularly for accessing my inner wisdom and answers. Whenever I was unsure about what to do, I activated my core and asked myself and then waited. The answer always came - sometimes from someone else, sometimes from an intuition or sudden insight, sometimes from another source such as a book or a sign from the universe.

Sometimes it came immediately and other times it took a while, so I remained patient, for it always came just at the right time. Peggy was right, the answers were indeed within me. I grew stronger in my self belief and self trust as I looked deeper and deeper within myself. Outside sources became less and less important. When I looked back at the days when I used to rely on friends, fortune tellers, 'channellings' and 'readings' to tell me what to do, I smiled to myself. I had come a long way since then!

Citizens of the Earth

Having grown up torn between two cultures, never feeling as if I belonged to either, I had dropped distinctions of country and culture early on in life. Later on though, through teaching English to people from a wide variety of social and cultural backgrounds, I did notice that there were indeed differences between people. Yet I still believed in everyone's equality. Equal but different was a concept that I couldn't quite explain to myself for a very long time. Looking to the Core Energy and the UCL allowed me to see both the equality and also the unique potentials everyone has - it gave me an explanation and a language for this idea. As Peggy says, "Celebrate the differences, but look to the unity." I now know how to do that.

A Way of Life

At first radiating my Core Energy was an exercise I did in times of need but as time went on, I integrated it more into my daily life and it became my intention to live in my core, to adopt this stance as a way of being. I familiarised myself with how it felt to be in that place and practised it daily. Gradually more and more of my life was spent living in my core and I knew immediately if I had come out of it - and that didn't matter, for I knew how to come back in!

Side Fibres - Finding the Balance

Becoming aware of the energy held in my side fibres and working with them made perhaps the most profound difference to my life. In every job I had ever had, I had always been unconsciously giving my energy away to colleagues, bosses and students. I took responsibility for everyone's emotions and opinions at work, for my self-worth was based on what they thought of me. I was constantly trying to please everyone and to keep everyone happy. And it was the same in my friendships and relationships - I often formed unhealthy attachments, becoming entangled with others to the extent where I couldn't see the line which separated my life from the other person's. This made me very tired. When I attempted to detach by keeping my distance, this would come across as me being hard hearted and cold. I was either all heart and no head or vice versa - I couldn't seem to get the balance right!

I was always rushing headlong into situations without considering the consequences. When things went wrong, I detached and rushed to the next relationship or job, the next best offer. There was no time to stop and think, no time to face up to what I was doing. I acted blindly and made decisions based purely on immediate survival. For a while it seemed as if I was neither head nor heart - I was just a zombie!

As I worked with the side fibres of my UCL, I understood why this was happening and why I had for so many years felt drained and unbalanced. The work helped to bring me into balance. My heart began to unfreeze and I began to use my mind to think about things before I took action - the two began to harmonise and I learned to make healthy decisions for myself. I also began to consciously call my energy back from tiring or draining situations. This allowed me to detach, but with grace and love. I then became more aware of exactly where my energy was going. And I made a conscious effort to actually choose what to give my energy to, instead of just unconsciously allowing it to go. Doing this was so liberating and I noticed that the dramas I had thrived on for so much of my life disappeared and life became so much easier, more stable and balanced. Doing this also trained me to become more discerning of others and how they were affecting my life. I learned to detect an unhealthy situation and rectify it. I had never felt so empowered.

Able To Be Alone

For the first time I felt happy in my own company. There was no longer any need to keep myself busy to avoid feeling what was within me or any need to create dramas to make my life interesting. The work gave me the courage to look deep within and be honest with myself. The cycle of destructive behaviour was well and truly over. My personal space for contemplation and creativity became both more precious and necessary.

Living in Synchronicity

I now have a unique and wondrous relationship with the universe. Answers, information, assistance and resources flow effortlessly to me at just the right time. The precision and clarity of the answers I receive is absolutely amazing and I often smile at how very personal to me they are! I am experiencing living 'under grace', enjoying each syncronicity, and marvelling at the incredible adventure my life has become. I have finally remembered the magic and wonder of life. The EMF Balancing Technique has helped me to remember what I had forgotten for so long.

The Infinite Possibilities of Who I Am

Personal Evolution

My personal growth continued in 2002 in many ways; I could feel that the evolution of who I really was deepened considerably during that year. Doing the work was activating latent talents, suppressed abilities and innate strengths - talents I never knew I had, or even imagined I could possibly have, emerged. I was finding out more and more about myself and I found myself doing things I would never have dreamed possible. These skills naturally and gradually emerged and evolved as time went by. I knew that the back of my UCL was unlocking these abilities with perfect timing in its usual self-regulating and self-directing way, making sure that I never had to cope with anything that was not appropriate for me. Events unfolded naturally and organically - and I was always quite able to handle them. Some things initially seemed like a bit of a challenge, but each time I got started, I tapped into an inner energy and I was carried along by the momentum. Once I had started, what I was doing suddenly felt completely natural to me. And afterwards I was elated - I had achieved something more. I was always amazed that I had actually achieved so many things and each time a part of me thought I had reached my final goal. But then new goals would emerge effortlessly, I would achieve them, and then the next goal would naturally arise. With each achievement I felt fuller and fuller, more and more 'me'. The real 'me', hidden away for so long out of fear and insecurity, started to blossom. And that 'me' was growing and evolving constantly.

A Golden Leap Forward

At the end of 2001, Michael and I taught Mark Goldie, a television editor, who suggested making an introductory video to the work. The aim was to show practitioners in the UK talking about how the work had affected them personally and also to show them performing some of the movements of the technique. This was an exciting project for us and we thoroughly enjoyed interviewing and filming. But never having talked to a camera before, I was afraid and kept putting off my turn to be filmed. In the end, though, once I started talking my nerves disappeared, I let go and something inside me clicked. I spoke from truth, from personal experience and the words flowed. Once we had finished filming our part, I felt a real sense of breakthrough. Something new opened up in me that day, a new confidence. It felt as if I had turned a corner. And more was to come.

Stepping Out

In the spring of 2002 Fiona House, a practitioner we had taught, suggested we give talks about the work at Watkins bookshop in central London where she was working, and arranged this for us. Stepping out of home and talking to groups of people in the UK's biggest and most well-known esoteric bookshop brought up more than a few fears for me! But yet again, once I started talking, another part of me emerged and the information flowed. We gave a series of talks and each time my voice became stronger and stronger. I was beginning to relate less and less to the shy and silent schoolgirl, sitting quietly listening in class. This felt more like who I was! Sitting on the tube on the way home after a particularly successful evening, I felt as if I had reached the pinnacle of my EMF career - there could be nothing more to achieve, surely? But there was.

Co-Teaching with Peggy Phoenix Dubro

During the summer of 2002 Michael and I were busy organising Peggy and Steve's UK autumn visit, during which Peggy was to teach a practitioner and a teacher training. Sometime during that summer, they invited us to co-teach with Peggy-

Peggy would teach the basic training and we would teach the advanced training. We were both overwhelmed to be offered this incredible opportunity. It would be our first time teaching more than six people and our first workshop out of home! Knowing that Michael and I would be doing this together, I had no nerves and was actually looking forward to it. However, the evening before we were due to teach, Michael became ill, too ill to teach the next day. It dawned on me that I was going to have to teach that day myself and I spent a restless night, worrying about this.

Photos by Jackie Calderwood

Standing in front of twenty people the next morning, my stomach churning, microphone in hand, explaining the work, writing on the flipchart, I felt as if I was in a dream. I was aware that people would be comparing me to Peggy and this scared me. In the end, I decided that the best tactic was to just be myself and do the job to the best of my abilities. It worked.

That evening at home I was completely exhausted, but proud of what I had achieved. It had been an awesome experience for me both personally and professionally. I had co-taught with Peggy Phoenix Dubro! I was immensely grateful to Peggy and Steve for this wonderful opportunity. To me this was ultimate proof that with a desire to learn and grow, coupled with the discipline to practise what you have learnt, you can achieve more than you ever imagined, no matter where you began from. In bed that night, my mind replayed some of the events of the year. A pattern emerged. My inner wisdom was guiding a process of activating innate talents and attracting opportunities for me to explore those talents, helping me to become more and more. This was what opening to the infinite possibilities of my being meant! I was a testimony to myself - you really can transform your life and you really can become who you would like to be.

The Energy Extension, Inc

Michael and I now work closely with Steve and Peggy and their team at The Energy Extension Inc. We are both honoured to work with a group of people of such high integrity, who embody their truth, are so gracious and work with a high standard of ethics. We respect Steve and Peggy for the kind of leadership they represent - for their hard work, dedication, co-operation and devotion. We are excited to be part of a company working in the new energy dynamics. Most of all, we are grateful to be working with people in the energy of love and empowerment.

Follow Your Dream and Be Yourself

The year 2002 presented me with many opportunities to learn and evolve, but the event I was to remember most vividly was the death of my father. My father had suffered from Crohn's disease for most of his life and in early 2002 his health began to deteriorate. By the spring his deterioration was serious and I eagerly offered him the four phases, happy to be able to help in some way, but he declined. The medication he had been given was having no effect, his condition was worsening and I could see that he was becoming desperate but was too proud to ask for help.

One morning in June, on a sudden impulse, I telephoned him. "Would you like to come over for some EMF sessions?" I asked. "I'll be there in ten minutes", he said. He had agreed - I couldn't believe it! I ran around preparing the room, putting some essential oils into the burner to create the most relaxing space I could. He arrived, took off his shoes, walked straight into the room and lay on the couch. I told him that I was going to give him a Phase One and Two combination EMF Balancing Technique session today and that tomorrow he was to come back for Phases Three and Four. "Ok", was all he said. I explained that I would be moving my hands within his energy field but that sometimes I would place my hands on his body. I told him that I was going to say some words aloud which may sound a little unusual to him, but that he should just relax. I then put some music on and began the session.

I could hardly believe that this was happening. It felt like a dream. The man I had hated so much throughout my life, the man I hardly knew, the man who had caused me so much grief, was accepting the work I loved so much. I looked at him lying on my couch and said the opening greeting, "From the Creator within me, to the Creator within you, and the company we keep, let us begin". As I spoke, I felt the overwhelming sensation of the energy of love and the full significance of those words suddenly hit me. It was as if I was understanding the real meaning for the first time. I looked at him lying on my couch, pale and weak, and I suddenly saw him as a part of the Creator. There was no more of God in me than in him - we were equal. I realised that no matter how he had behaved towards me until that point, at his core he was as much a piece of the Creator as anyone else. Until now I had only seen his sadness, anger and frustration, those emotions that were layered over his true essence. It felt as if those layers were now stripped away and we were going to communicate core to core. We had stepped into a whole new and different dimension, one where we were not just father and daughter, but two humans working together in love. I had said those words to my clients countless times, but only now did I feel the full impact of their true meaning.

As I progressed with the session I began to feel an overwhelming energy of unconditional love and compassion for him. Working through his UCL I sensed his anger and also his sadness. For the first time in my life my heart opened to him. As I worked through the back of his UCL I sensed all the experiences of his history. My father's personality receded and I became aware of him as just a person, a client, a human being, a man just like any other.

It was an enormous experience for me. I had taken a step back and I was able to see him objectively and understand so much about him. I saw how his thoughts and emotions had shaped my life and I understood the role he had played in my growth. I somehow had a sense of the lineage I had been born into. And I could feel myself forgiving him. The room was full with the energy of love. I knew that this was a unique experience for me and that I should savour every moment. I gave him the session with tears streaming down my face. Every single word I said was poignant and seemed to come alive with its full significance for both of us.

At the end of the session, with one hand on his heart and one hand on the back of his neck, I spoke the closing ceremony - "Peter, be aware of your light and energy......". I had never addressed him by his first name before but now it was appropriate - he was a human being, a person in his own right, not just 'my father'. As I said the final words, "I honour you and the Creator within you", I truly meant them. He seemed very peaceful after the session and thanked me. Even though I knew that the outcome would be directed by his inner wisdom for his highest good, I prayed for a miracle.

The next morning he returned. There was something very different about him. He asked about my work, about how it was going and seemed to actually be listening to what I said. He was much more talkative and much more natural with me. He told me that he had been sceptical of this work before but that he now completely believed in it. I was amazed at the transformation. He lay on the couch and I began the session. Within twenty minutes he became very ill and I had to keep stopping the session to attend to him. He suggested that maybe we should stop and finish off some other time, but something told me that there might not be another time - this had to be done now. He could not lie down, so I asked him to sit up and I talked him through the rest of the session. He went home and again I prayed for a miracle.

Two hours later I received a call from my sister. He had deteriorated so much that he had been admitted to hospital. He was to stay in hospital for two months. I visited him every day, staying with him for up to nine hours at a time. For the first time in my life my father was actually happy to see me and he began to talk to me. He told me about his life and asked me about mine. For much of this time I was in complete shock and it passed by in a haze. I wasn't used to this kind of relationship and I was often so stunned by what was happening that I gave merely monosyllabic answers. For the next month the most amazing transformation took place within my father and in our relationship. Although he never actually apologised for the way he had behaved towards me, I understood that this was what he was trying to do. I could sense his regret and remorse and I was aware that he could not let his mask of survival drop, even for a moment. He wanted nothing to come between us, now that we were so close, he told me. He intended to make amends and begin a proper family life. Now that he had seen how it was possible to change your life for the better, he said, he wanted to go home to do it and he listed all the changes he was going to make in his life. When I left the hospital in the evenings, he would often tell me that he would be thinking about me all night. To these comments I often just stared at him, mute. I still couldn't take in what was happening. An incredible spiritual transformation was taking place for my father and it was all such a shock for me.

A month after being admitted to hospital, he deteriorated so much that he was transferred to intensive care. There he was completely sedated, as he underwent life-saving operation after life-saving operation. The next few weeks were very stressful and he was constantly on the verge of death. However, he somehow managed to survive and one day the doctors told us that he was out of danger and that his sedation would be gradually lessened so that he could wake up. He did awaken slightly but to my disappointment, he never really recognised any of us. I felt I had so quickly lost the precious new relationship that had begun to develop between us and I was very sad. But I was wrong, it had not been lost, for one day I went into his room and saw that he had managed to write some words on a piece of paper. Those words were "Lina, Lina, Lina". The next day a nurse asked me if I knew who Lina was - Mr Esposito kept asking for her. Excitedly, I rushed over to his bed and spoke to him, but still he did not recognise me. I was saddened, but now I knew that our new connection was not lost, it was still there, deep within him. A week later he died. My family and I never got to have that new life together, but I feel blessed to have been a part of my father's incredible spiritual transformation and to have been able to enjoy a new, if somewhat brief, relationship with him.

Giving my father EMF Balancing Technique sessions was one of the most poignant moments of my whole life. Those sessions were the only chance I ever got to have some sort of personal bond with him, the only time I ever touched him, the only time I ever related to him adult to adult. Peggy Phoenix Dubro often talks about the importance of us honouring each other, human to human. I now have proof that this is possible, no matter what each of those humans have been through together. Working with this energy has enabled me to honour and respect my father for who he was, in spite of the challenges we have been through. The sessions did not bring about his physical healing, but they sparked a rapid spiritual transformation within him and our relationship that I would never have dreamed possible. I was amazed at how quickly we had achieved this together and how effortlessly - proof again that this new energy and this new way of working is so very gentle and graceful yet so incredibly fast.

A few months later I had a vivid dream in which my father told me "Follow your dream and be yourself." I knew those were two things he never had the courage to do and I sensed his deep regret. The EMF Balancing Technique has enabled me to take that advice and put it into practice in my own life. It is my wish that this book will help you to find your dream, follow it, and be yourself.

Dedication

I have felt my father's presence and support whilst writing this book and by a wonderful synchronicity, I finished the main text on the anniversary of his death - 9th August 2003. As I typed in the very last word, my sister called to tell me that she and my mother were making their way to the cemetery to visit his grave. I left home and joined them. Laying our flowers at his grave, I caught sight of the time - it was ten to two, exactly the time he had passed away.

A few days after my father's death, whilst looking through his belongings, I found in his wallet a poem he had written many years earlier. As I read through it, I felt a powerful energy surge through my body and a strong sense of his presence. Later, when I found a few more copies of it around the house, I realised that it must have been his favourite poem.

I feel that my father is now with me - more than he ever was when he was alive. I know that he has been helping me to write this book and I include his poem on the next page as a tribute to him and for you to enjoy.

Burnham Beeches

These dreams
that divide the evening air,
rise like spent candlesmoke in unspoken prayer.

Wandering in the eaves,
of a cathedral of tall beech trees,
hoisted by a silver thread
I look down to see my body, spread.

Pale and empty
on a couch of copper leaves,
that only last October were dropped as golden coins
to stay Winter's first frosty breath,
and only brought three days
of distant sun that did not even colour
Autumn's death,
I saw my own faint misty breath.

There is no pain floating here
but, caught in evening's ambush,
my body fades.
Nightcalls, that string the silence with
imagined heartbeats,
echo loudly through the moonshadowed
glades, of my mind.

Long ago,
with wax-wings, Icarus flew blindly
towards the sun,
and being soul-less fell.
But here, climbing the creaming cloudfall,
my silver thread
collects the dew-pearls of all the mornings of
my life
and whirls them, flashing moon-fire,
through my head.

To suddenly awake in the soft English
rain beneath Burnham Beeches.

By *Peter Esposito*
26th April 1935 - 9th August 2002

Further Reading

Peggy Phoenix Dubro and *David Lapierre*
Elegant Empowerment: Evolution of Consciousness
Platinum Publishing House

Robert O. Becker, M.D. and *Gary Selden*
The Body Electric: Electromagnetism and the Foundation of Life
Quill

Robert O. Becker, M.D.
Cross Currents: The Perils of Electropollution, The Promise of
Electromedicine
Tarcher Putnam

Kryon Book Seven
Letters from Home: Loving Messages from the Family
The Kryon Writings, Inc.

Gregg Braden
Awakening to Zero Point: The Collective Initiation
Radio Bookstore Press

Caroline Myss PH.D
Why People Don't Heal and How They Can
Bantam Books

Blair Justice, PH.D
A different Kind of Health: Finding Well-being Despite Illness
Peak Press

Mark Greenia, M.A
Energy Dynamics: Conscious Human Evolution
Unlimited Publishing

Brian Greene
The Elegant Universe: Superstrings, Hidden Dimensions and the
Quest for the Ultimate Theory

Index

Contact Information

For more information on becoming an *EMF Balancing Technique*® practitioner or teacher, and for a worldwide schedule of classes please visit the official EMF website:

www.EMFWorldwide.com

You can also contact Energy Extension, Inc.

The Energy Extension, Inc.
P.O. Box 4357, Sedona AZ, USA 86340
Phone: +1-928-284-3703 **Fax:** +1-928-284-3704
Email: Shana@EMFWorldwide.com

To Contact The Author
You may contact Lina Esposito by writing to:
Email: LinaEsposito@aol.com

For *EMF Balancing Technique*® teaching schedules in the UK & Ireland please visit the official EMF website:

www.emfbalancingtechnique.co.uk

Email:
LifeForceEMF@aol.com
Phone:
EMF Infoline (UK freephone): 0800 085 3765
International: +44 20 8349 1544

Other Books from Platinum Publishing

Elegant Empowerment -
An Evolution of Consciousness
Peggy Phoenix Dubro and David Lapierre

A breakthrough book merging Science and Spirituality. Important information for understanding the human energy anatomy.

Whether your interest is motivational, psychological, spiritual or scientific, **Elegant Empowerment** takes you on a journey of accelerated personal transformation. This is the first book to document the structure and scientific basis of the **Universal Calibration Lattice® (UCL)**. A unique geometric & harmonic configuration of light & sound, the UCL is a vital system within the human energy anatomy.

"Now is the perfect time to discover for yourself the power of the UCL and learn more about the EMF Balancing Technique to achieve greater balance and freedom in your life... Refer to this book often, it is a foundational guide for further discovery on our collective evolutionary path."

Lee Carroll Best selling author of KRYON Book series, and co-author Indigo Children books

ISBN 0-9711074-0-8 • $22.00

To read excerpts from the book, please visit
www.ElegantEmpowerment.com

Wellness with Tachyon - (To be published in 2005!)
Galaxy Nº 1 - Tommy Thomsen and Martina Bochnik

"What can I say? I'm sold! Over the years, when I didn't have the device around, I missed it! It seemed to have a very calming attribute about it, almost like it was a partner ... but yet only a piece of colored glass? No. Much, much more.

I believe Tachyon energy is the beginning of the kind of cooperation between Humanity and Universal energy that we have been waiting for. It indeed is a helpful bridge of intelligent energy that seems to know exactly what we need. It's not invasive, but cooperative. It's a sweet, powerful energy that I've come to respect and love to be around. I call it 'personal energy'."

Thank you Tommy and Martina, for your work in helping to expose this wonderful new energy to our planet!"

Lee Carroll Best selling author of KRYON Book series, and co-author Indigo Children books

Other Related Products and Information

The Universal Calibration Lattice Tape set or CD set

The tape set and CD set include a booklet complete with illustrations for each part of the Mini Session. You can learn to do this session!

Tape #1 or CD #1: Introduction (60 min)
Learn about the Universal Calibration Lattice, a system in the human energy anatomy composed of fibers of light and energy. Understand the pattern these fibers create and the energetic framework they provide.

Tape #2 or CD #2: Spiral Sweep - Mini Energy Session (60 min)
Side (a) - Explore the connection between the endocrine system and the chakras. Strengthen your inner balance with a unique energy exercise called the Spiral Sweep.

Side (b) - Hear step-by-step instructions on tape while following illustrations in the booklet as you learn to perform the graceful movements of the EMF Balancing Technique® Mini Session.   ISBN 0-9711074-1-6 ● $18.00

I Remember I Am Meditation 2 CD set (80 min)

Peggy Phoenix Dubro skillfully combines unique meditations, energetic exercises, and selected readings from her book **Elegant Empowerment**. Designed to increase understanding of our sacredness as unique individuals and our connection with one another, this loving offering of practical advice and profound meditations create an exceptional CD experience. **Dedicated to the Creator within YOU!**

ISBN 0-9711074-2-4 ● $18.00

Attributes of Mastery Cards

From the beginning of civilization, spiritual mastery has been surrounded in mystery and ceremony. Now the secret is out ... you can PRACTICE mastery in your everyday life! In this box you will find our first offering of **44 Attributes of Mastery,** their definitions, and a booklet with simple instructions to assist as you PRACTICE mastery. I know you already possess these attributes of mastery, and many more. These cards are an invitation to encourage the expression of these attributes, and to increase your ability to co-create an enlightened life in accordance with your innermost, innate, and most wonderful wisdom. Think of what living in mastery means to you and **PRACTICE**.   ISBN 0-9711074-5-9 ● $22.00

In the Energy of Love,   Also available *International Card Deck* - 4 languages
Peggy Phoenix Dubro   in one set: English, German, French, Spanish!

For a complete list of products please visit our on-line store at:
www.EMFWorldwide.com
or call us at Tel: **+1-928-284-3703** Fax: **+1-928-284-3704**
Energy Extension, Inc. P.O. Box 4357, Sedona AZ, USA 86340